Exotic Needlework

with Ethnic Patterns, Techniques, Inspirations

ART-CRAFT BOOKS BY DONA Z. MEILACH

FIBERS AND FABRICS

Contemporary Batik and Tie-Dye
Contemporary Leather
Creating Art from Fibers and Fabrics
Creative Stitchery *with Lee Erlin Snow*
Macramé Accessories
Macramé: Creative Design in Knotting
Making Contemporary Rugs and Wall Hangings
A Modern Approach to Basketry with Fibers and Grasses
Plant Hangers
Soft Sculpture and Other Soft Art Forms
Weaving Off-Loom *with Lee Erlin Snow*

SCULPTURE

Contemporary Art with Wood
Contemporary Stone Sculpture
Creating Art with Bread Dough
Creating Modern Furniture
Creating Small Wood Objects as Functional Sculpture
Creating with Plaster
Creative Carving
Decorative and Sculptural Ironwork
Direct Metal Sculpture *with Donald Seiden*
Sculpture Casting *with Dennis Kowal*

COLLAGE-PAPER

Accent on Crafts
Box Art: Assemblage and Construction
Collage and Assemblage *with Elvie Ten Hoor*
Collage and Found Art *with Elvie Ten Hoor*
Creating Art from Anything
Papercraft
Papier-Mâché Artistry
Printmaking

DESIGN

The Artist's Eye
How to Create Your Own Designs *with Jay and Bill Hinz*

Also

The Art of Belly Dancing *with Dahlena*
Jazzercise *with Judi Missett*

Exotic Needlework

with Ethnic Patterns, Techniques, Inspirations

by DONA Z. MEILACH and DEE MENAGH

Photography: Dona and Mel Meilach
Drawings: Dee Menagh

CROWN PUBLISHERS, INC., NEW YORK

Dedicated to
John and Sophie Smith

Inquiries should be addressed to Crown Publishers, Inc., One Park Avenue,
New York, N.Y. 10016

Printed in the United States of America

Published simultaneously in Canada by
General Publishing Company Limited

Book Design: Shari de Miskey

Design Consultant: Dona Z. Meilach

Library of Congress Cataloging in Publication Data
Meilach, Dona Z
Exotic needlework, with ethnic patterns, techniques,
trends.
Bibliography: p.
Includes index.
1. Needlework.   2. Embroidery.   3. Design,
Decorative.   I. Menagh, Dee, joint author.   II. Title.
TT751.M35 1978   746.4   78-932
ISBN 0-517-52953-X
ISBN 0-517-52954-8 pbk.

Acknowledgments

We are sincerely grateful to the needleworkers, past and present, known and unknown by name, whose work is included in this book. We apologize for the anonymity of people from various corners of the earth; we respect them and their generosity for posing and proudly showing their handwork for our cameras.

We especially want to thank General Lowell E. English, USMC (Ret.), director of the San Diego Museum of Man, and the staff, for their cooperation and permission to cull from their collection and photograph items that would underscore the concepts we are presenting. We appreciate all the assistance of the Field Museum of Natural History, Chicago, Illinois, and the Milwaukee Public Museum, Milwaukee, Wisconsin, for access to their collections.

Our thanks too, to the private collectors who welcomed us and discussed their prized possessions with us. We especially wish to extend our appreciation and admiration to Diane Powers of the Bazaar del Mundo, Old Town, San Diego, California, for permitting us full acess to her marvelous collection of fabrics, costumes, and clothing.

Our thanks to all the artists who entrusted us with their handmade wear and to the models who donned the wild and wonderful pieces, helped carry them so carefully to various photography sites, and changed their clothing in hot cars and trailers.

We will be forever grateful to our husbands who assisted in ways too numerous to list them all. Mel Meilach lugged cameras and waited patiently, stoically, while we arranged folds and gathers until they were exactly right for photography. He is responsible for all photos in Guatemala, taken while he was voluntarily helping at dental clinics in different parts of that country. Dave Menagh added large doses of moral support, amusement, and encouragement whenever our energies lagged, and closed his eyes at the disarray of his home turned into a photography studio and setting for wall hangings, draped yardage, and models.

We appreciate the expertise and efficiency of Collette Russell, who helped with the hundreds of letters and photographs submitted by craftspeople all over the country, and to Marilyn Regula for her splendid job of typing the final manuscript.

Anyone interested in contacting people whose work is shown in the book for exhibitions, commissions, or workshops, should send a stamped, self-addressed envelope to the authors, care of Crown Publishers, Inc., One Park Ave., New York, New York 10016.

Dona Meilach and Dee Menagh
San Diego, California

Note: Photographs, unless otherwise credited, are by Dona and Mel Meilach.

Contents

1. Needlework Around the World

THE NEEDLE, PROBABLY THE SIMPLEST TOOL KNOWN TO MAN, IS possibly one of the oldest. It is easy to use, incredibly versatile. And how we take it for granted! Despite its long history in every world culture, there are innumerable innovative ways it can still be used by the creative person to explore hundreds of new horizons.

The needle, whether made of bone, tendons, or steel, has been used to join materials and embellish them since primitive peoples sewed skins together and found they could make a pattern of their stitches. Ancient Egyptians embroidered linen garments. The tribes of Israel embroidered tent hangings. Both Aristotle (third century B.C.) and Pliny (first century A.D.) describe methods of obtaining silk and spinning a fine thread. Silk for weaving and decorating has a history that winds all the way back to ancient China. American Indians evolved elaborate patterns by sewing beads on animal skins. During the Middle Ages, needlework was a highly developed art practiced by the nuns and by ladies in castles who embroidered rich designs for church altars, priests' robes, and regal garments to be used on state occasions.

The history of needlework during the pre- and post-Christian eras is lost or vague in many countries where high humidity has ravaged the perishable materials. The earliest fragments are those that were preserved in the dry Egyptian tombs. Evidence indicates that plain woven materials appeared first, followed by painted designs about 2500 B.C., and embroidery after that. The process of weaving a design in cloth itself probably was not developed until much later. Knowledge of ancient fibers and cloth varies considerably because remnants found on archeological sites are not always reliable examples of the variety or quantity of textiles in use at a particular time.

Decorated textiles have a fascinating history, and possibly this book will lead you to explore areas of special interest to you. We will not attempt, in this discussion, to cover needlework history nor to show every technique used in every country; that would be an encyclopedic undertaking. Our purpose is to make you aware of and to show how you can borrow and be inspired by patterns, motifs, modes of dress, and colors from peoples at any time, ancient or modern, from any type of cultural background.

Spanish Shawl. Silk threads on silk crepe. Chinese motifs worked by Chinese embroiderers in Manila, the Philippines, ca. 1910
Collection, William S. Chandler
San Diego, California

1

Skirt border (detail). Birds and flowers worked mainly in the long stitch on a ground of hand-spun and hand-woven cotton. Nahua Indian, Acatlan, Guerrero, Mexico.

Photographed at
San Diego Museum of Man

A woman's platform shoe from China is embroidered with light thread on dark ground and the reverse, dark thread on light ground. Included is the "Pekinese" stitch, which probably originated in China. The stitch is illustrated on page 21.

Photographed at
San Diego Museum of Man

Our urge to create and embellish with needle and thread reflects an age-old impulse to decorate. In our present mass-production society there is a need to feel unique, to avoid uniformity. There are infinite ways to adapt ideas from everywhere to make them individually yours, even if this is the first time you are threading a needle. You don't need a large vocabulary of techniques. Often stunning results are achieved with simple tools, materials, and stitches. It's fun to know many stitches, but the final results depend on how creatively you use those you know, rather than on the variety employed.

Until recently, fashion was dictated by a small group of couturiers whose ideas were slavishly copied, modified, mass-produced, and foisted upon the public. In our era these dictates are lost in the winds. Freedom and individuality are the high style notes: freedom to wear clothes that make us comfortable; freedom to delve into styles from every corner of the earth, to go wild for the wonderful exuberant designs of folk people, of picturesque village costumes, of a whole new way of dressing up or dressing casually. It has opened our eyes to new ideas for decorating our rooms and giving our environments greater pizzazz, greater interest.

The "ethnic" look does not mean that you will be mistaken for a coolie plucking rice from the paddies, a nomad in the desert, or a peasant selling wares at an open market. Ethnic clothing styles and decorations are not meant to be copied exactly as would a historian or a theatrical costume designer for a period stage production. The concept is to adapt the patterns, designs, and techniques to contemporary usage so they will be attractive, yet different. They are aimed to give you a sense of "oneness"...the only one to wear what *you* are wearing and to look the way *you* do in it.

All the ideas offered in the following pages can be styled differently to make them sophisticated or casual, subdued or bold, as your tastes prefer. One simple pattern, for example, can be altered tremendously by changing fabrics, colors, detailing, or portions of the garment. You may like the bodice from one, the neckline from another, the sleeves from still another. You may like one pattern from a North African dress, then prefer a surface embellishment suggested by a different country. The same basic pattern may be changed so many ways that it appears to be a different dress with infinite variety each time it is made. You are free to select, then assemble any of the elements into a delightful medley of styling. If it fits your figure or your total scheme of decorating it is right for you and that makes it right!

Some fabric and fashion designers have already spotted this exotic trend, and you can take advantage of it in several ways:

First: Printed and dyed yard goods that echo the colors and designs of other cultures are becoming more readily available. You will find marvelous fabrics with large geometric patterns in earth colors based on American Indian blankets. There are small printed designs with self-borders of crisscrosses, stripes, triangles, and squares that may be straight out of a Slavic countryside. You may flip for the assorted prints as dizzying and dramatic as the Turkish rug that inspired them. Use these prints for entire outfits, for portions of them, or for trim.

Second: Pattern companies such as Vogue, Simplicity, Butterick, and McCall's have observed the pendulum swinging to this free-style movement. They are beginning to offer a few patterns adapted from costumes of other countries. The copy may note that a pattern "is a takeoff of a Russian peasant blouse and that the inserts suggested for the bib and sleeves are reminiscent of traditional Russian embroidery." The pattern may include a transfer design so you can emulate the embroidery, if you like.

A new pattern company, Folkwear, anticipated a strong demand for ethnic clothing. They developed a line of patterns with authentically styled garments from other countries that would be practical for today's fashion-conscious seamstress and with modifications for contemporary life-styles. Each pattern offers variations for embellishing the garment that you may follow or alter. A Turkish coat, for example, can be made of an outer layer of any fabric you like such as lightweight wool, silk, broadcloth, percale, or linen, quilted cotton, or lightweight permanent-press fabrics. The border suggestions include a series of handmade trapunto zigzag designs, or you can substitute commercially quilted fabrics. You might prefer a band of brightly embroidered flowers inspired by Mexican blouses or cross stitching drafted from Yugoslavian linens. One could also add rows of buttons and silver dangles seen in the trim on Yemenite clothing. Or the entire coat could be made of Oriental prints and paisleys without additional trim.

Third: For those who may not like to sew the basic pattern, the ethnic look can still be yours. Old and new ready-made clothing and objects can be changed dramatically with the addition of some detailing from another culture. A pillow cover embroidered in India with hundreds of stitches and scores of shi sha mirrors can be refashioned as a capelet or bib with or

A beaded square with geometric animals and trees and a stylized border design from India is the center of a fabric panel that might be used for a pillow cover or purse front.
Collection, Mr. & Mrs. Wayne Chapman, Solana Beach, California

Sequins and gold thread couched to a black cotton material, with appliqué and embroidery. Simple techniques add up to an interesting composition in a wall panel from Burma, probably late nineteenth-century.

Collection, Julanna Loveberg El Cajon, California

Beading has been, and still is, used by many cultures in traditional designs but with extremely varied results. A Thai needleworker (Meo Hill tribe area) strings beads to be used for decorations on an embroidered hat.

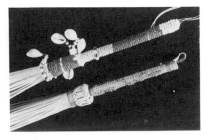

Fly whisks probably made by the Seminole Indians of Florida. Beaded lengths are worked around a handle.
Photographed at
San Diego Museum of Man

A blouse from Poland has Cross-Stitch embroidery on the sleeves combined with a crocheted collar and crocheted lace-trim cuffs. It illustrates how different techniques can be effectively combined.
Photographed at Milwaukee Public Museum, Milwaukee, Wisconsin by Dale D. Menagh

without new elements added; it will change the look of any sweater or blouse instantly and dramatically. A basic overblouse can be "ethnicized" by appliqués of lace doilies with beads added, or by layering preprinted ribbons and adding tassels. A cotton blue-jean shirt or pants can become elegant with a richly embroidered symbol freely adapted from an Indian artifact and developed in "reverse appliqué"—a technique raised to a high level of craftsmanship by the Cuna Indians of Central America.

In the following chapters you will discover hundreds of ideas for making things from scratch, for embellishing the things you have, for buying things and making them better, for taking apart, reassembling and elaborating. You will find needlework techniques and patterns with which to use them. The basic embroidery stitches are shown, not with pointless samplers to practice them on, but with thoughtfully designed motifs developed from objects in various cultures. Each motif provides a design that you can apply to trim a shirt, skirt, purse, room accessory, or whatever you like.

You will become aware of the inspirations for design used by artists and craftsmen everywhere in every medium; they will wind up your own designer gears and set them whirring. You will observe how the stone carving on an Aztec calendar became a needlework motif for an elegant cape, how traditional Indian quillwork inspired a spectacular body covering made with plastic tubing; how nineteenth-century quilting was developed into a soft sculpure.

Then, when you begin to observe designs in books, magazines, and museums, you will discover that the same symbols occur again and again with slight variations. The Peruvians, the Greeks, the Indians, use the same patterns in different forms. There are motifs in Chinese patterns that are completely Celtic, such as dragons and twisted curling lines. Scandinavian designs came from China across the trade routes in Asia and Peru. In eighteenth-century Europe designs that were brought in from the East were so much in vogue that they were applied in painting, dishes,

clothing; the word "chinoiserie," which means "in the Chinese manner," describes that trend.

Investigating ethnic sources for needlework provides another bonus: you'll learn a marvelous vocabulary of clothing styles. For instance:

The "pareu" is a wraparound skirt from Polynesia that can be used for a bathing suit cover-up or for a formal skirt.

A "huipil" is a specially designed overblouse from Guatemala usually made of three breadths of fabric and woven on the loom. It may be short, exposing some midriff, or long and coatlike with variations in length. It can be worn tucked into a skirt or allowed to slap loosely. Its pattern, whether brocaded or stitched, varies from village to village.

A "quechquemitl" is an upper garment that gives the effect of a cape with triangles over the chest and back, and is known nowhere else in the world except Central America, almost entirely in Mexico.

The "capexii," an outer garment worn by the men of Mexico and Guatemala, combines the elements of a jacket and a serape. It is a rectangle of heavy felted wool, doubled over with a slit for the head, with two sleeves sewn on. The sides are stitched together only to the armpit which is left open to allow freedom of movement.

The "sarafan," a national dress of Russia, is a loose-fitting jumper with narrow shoulder straps worn over a peasant-style blouse tied at the neck. The style is ageless, handed down from mother to daughter for holiday festivities. Because sarafans are not subject to style changes they are often given hours of loving, imaginative embroidery. They are worn over layers of skirts that are embellished with woven braids and trims.

You may find it exciting, too, to learn why certain designs have become part of a particular country's folklore. The embroidery designs on nineteenth-century Welsh smocks were often symbols that denoted a person's type of work. Young Anatolian girls, even today, express their emotions with needle and thread, as did their grandmothers. A girl who sends her young man a handkerchief embroidered in yellow is telling him

The typical clothing worn by the men of Santiago Atitlan, Guatemala, includes hand-woven purple and white striped pants with intricate hand embroidery around each leg at the knee.
Photo, Mel Meilach

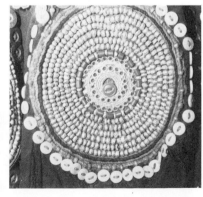

Beads and coins in a circular design from a Yemenite garment can suggest ideas for embellishing clothes and furnishings.
Photo, Dee Menagh
Dress, Collection, Stana Coleman,
Evanston, Illinois

Long Satin Stitches characterize the work on a huipil of the Tzeltal Indians of Chiapas, Mexico.
Photographed at
San Diego Museum of Man

A fetish shirt worn by an African tribesman is laden with rectangular mirrors, which are believed to ward off evil spirits. In India, shi sha mirrors, which are small, round, or square, serve mainly as decoration in a hot, drab climate.
Collection, Roger Brown, Chicago

she is in love. A bride who wears a scarf with green stitching is saying, "I like my new home and I get along with the family as smoothly as green grass."

Whether you have held a needle and thread in your hand for simple mending or for advanced needlework, you will find in every chapter a wellspring of ideas that you can apply for years. The garments and accessories were made by people just like you and photographed especially for this book. Some of the people were experienced needleworkers seeking new outlets for their talents and time. Others were learning the fundamentals of needlework and, after a few classes and some bad and some good starts, their patience paid off in results they were proud to use.

The examples illustrated may be copied or they may serve as suggestions, as jumping-off points for your own creativity. There are basics, how-to's, and designs to get you going. Use them to make your wardrobe, your family's wardrobe, and your home absolutely and uniquely yours. Use them to make gifts. Use them to appreciate materials and designs in shops that feature fabrics, objects, and ideas from all over the world. Use them to expand your interest in the world whether you travel extensively or stay at home. Use them to dig into current literature to learn about the lore and lure of people everywhere.

Brilliant and intricate embroidery in reds and purples characterizes a skirt border from an eighteenth-century Crete garment. Almost all space is filled with symbolic images (detail).
Courtesy, The Art Institute of Chicago

Opposite page:
In many countries, an enthusiasm for the needle is nurtured at an early age. In Hong Kong it is part of the curriculum of all primary and secondary school children. This young girl from the Meo Hill country of northern Thailand imitates her tribespeople in the costume and silver jewelry she wears and in her embroidery.

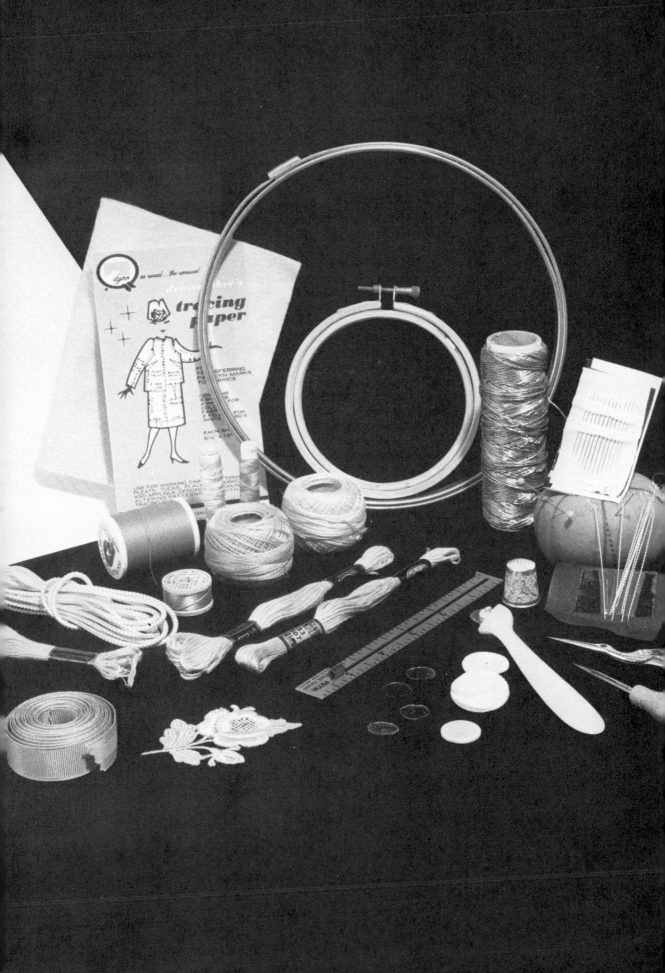

2. For A Starter—Basics

MATERIALS

THE MATERIALS YOU WILL NEED FOR YOUR OWN APPLICATION OF exotic ideas are not much different from those used by the very cultures you may study. Essentially, people work with what they have available—and it's hard to think of a better way to begin. Luckily, the availability of threads, needles, fabrics, and other embroidery accessories is as close as your sewing and needlework store. No need to card your own wool and spin your own threads, to make needles from bones as people once did (and probably still do) in many primitive societies. You can use what you have at hand, or easily buy materials you think will work best for a specific project.

It is always a good habit to stitch a small sample of the work to be sure the threads are compatible with the backing materials and to test its "in use" potential. Washable fabrics used for backing should be preshrunk so that shrinking will not cause threads to pucker the material. You should use the best quality threads you can buy, especially when scores of sewing hours and high hopes are involved in a project. Inferior threads may tend to fray from working and with wear; threads that are not colorfast can run onto fabrics and fade.

High-quality craftsmanship is a worthwhile goal. Evenly made stitches, straight seams, and interesting joinings all add immeasurably to the way the inside as well as the outside of your clothing feels and looks. A garment will reflect your work and your taste. Linings should be coordinated with the fabric exterior, and the attention to fine detail and finishing will make the pieces more precious and more valuable. Diane Garick Mergenov, whose wall hangings and garments are shown in chapters three and four, probably wins our top vote for fine finishing. All items are hand-sewn. Detailing at top of skirt slits repeats the outer designs. All are beautifully stitched onto carefully fitted linings. Hems are perfectly finished. The jacket necklines and inner flaps are works of art in themselves, so they look as lovely when they are off as when they are being worn.

Materials for embroidery include hoops, yarns and thread, pins, needles, pin-cushion, scissors, tracing and graph paper, a tracing wheel, and any sewing item that you may find adaptable to specific projects.

9

A basketful of Guatemalan and Mexican fabrics to be used for clothing embellishment.

Fabrics

The variety of fabrics readily available may make selection as difficult as a child's dilemma at a candy counter. Fortunately, linens, cottons, wools, silks, velvet, synthetics, and blends in a vast assortment of prints and solids and colors are all adaptable to the needlework fashions illustrated. In the ethnic idiom, you can hardly go wrong with any choice; for "ethnic" echoes "folkwear"—a hearty, outgoing approach to materials where prints are mated with other prints; where bold colors and exuberant designs reflect a vibrant spirit. Fabric selection will depend on your tastes—if you like it, wear it—and on the season or climate in which it is to be worn.

Select dress and upholstery fabrics, bed and table linens, new or used. Many of the garments begin with printed tablecloths, bedspreads, and yard goods known, because of their unique patterning and textures, to have been made in other countries. Bed linens today often have prints that can become beautiful backgrounds for additional embroidery and embellishments, and are a good buy for the quality and amount of fabric in them.

When imported fabrics are not readily available, use portions of material culled from clothing that may be found in garage sales and secondhand stores. Travelers often buy things on trips that never look quite right when they return home and which end up in resale shops. The practiced eye will quickly ferret out such items for recycling into unusual ethnic designs.

Threads and Yarns

Threads used for embroidery may be as fine and delicate as a spider's web or as textured and thick as rug yarn. Threads and yarns are generally attached through the backing material using a needle; but this is not always true. Thicker yarns can be placed on top of the fabric and "couched" or held to the material by holding it down with a thinner thread that is sewn through the material. Some threads may be punched through with a special needle or worked through the backing in a Chain Stitch with a crochet hook.

There are so many possibilities that one needs only to survey the sewing and needlework counters to find enough materials to begin practicing the stitches that follow. The threads you select are much like a painter's box of paints; with them you create the colors, the textures, the embellishments you visualize.

Embroidery threads are available mostly in balls, single-strand spools, and six-strand skeins. There are mercerized cottons and silks, in shiny and dull finish, and plain and twisted threads. Look also for carpet thread, polyester sewing threads, crewel, knitting, and crochet yarns, craft yarns, and novelty yarns. Linear designs using metal threads inventively are described in Chapter 6.

When you purchase colored yarns and embroidery threads, always buy enough for a given project because dye lots tend to vary if the same colors are purchased at different times. In many brands the color is designated by a three-digit number.

Embroidery-thread-size numbering may vary by manufacturer and in different countries, but generally, the larger the number, the thinner the thread.

Needles

Four types of needles are generally used for embroidery:

Sharps needles, medium length, have small eyes for sewing cotton or single strands of six-strand floss.

Embroidery (also called crewel) needles are numbered from 1 to 10 with No. 1 the thickest and longest (about 2 inches), and No. 10 the finest (1½ inches long).

Chenille needles range from No. 13, which is 2½ inches long and quite thick, to the finer No. 26, which is 1¼ inches long. They have large eyes for threading thick threads.

Tapestry needles have blunt tips and very large eyes; they are used for whipped stitches, needlepoint, and drawn-fabric and drawn-thread work. The largest, No. 13, is 2¾ inches long, and the finest, No. 26, is 1¼ inches long.

Select a needle that makes a clear opening in the fabric for the thickness of the thread that will be pulled through. If your thread breaks, your needle is probably too thin. If your stitching is uneven, and you are using a fairly thin thread, the needle may be too big. Sharp-pointed needles are used in most embroidery work; blunt-tip tapestry needles are handy for stitches to be woven on the surface of the material as they do not split the threads or catch on the backing fabric. When a sharp needle dulls from constant use, throw it away so you don't pick it up again.

Other Items

You will find the following to be useful: small sharp scissors, straight pins, beeswax to rub on threads so they will pull through more readily, thimble, and items illustrated on the following pages for stretching materials and tracing designs.

THREADING THE NEEDLE

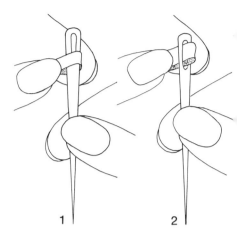

1 2

1. Fold the thread about 4 inches from end. Hold it taut and rub the fold up and down the needle.
2. Hold the thread near the fold. Push the needle eye onto the folded part and push thread through.

When multiple strands thwart needle-threading, place the thread ends in a folded piece of paper and push the paper through the needle eye. Or you can use a needle threader or a length of fine wire.

STARTING AND ENDING THREAD

To avoid a lumpy knot on the fabric underside, leave a tail of thread and finish by threading the end under the stitches. Heavy thread ends may be secured with fabric glue.

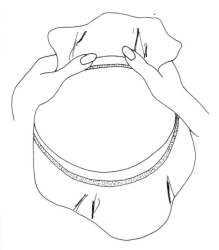

Fabric is usually woven with vertical and horizontal threads. When you place fabric between the rings of the hoop, pull it taut but keep the woven threads straight and at right angles to one another. Small embroidery hoops may have springs on the outer ring; larger hoops have screws to adjust to accommodate different thicknesses of materials.

Hoops and Frames

Hoops are composed of two parts with an adjustable spring or screw to allow for different fabric thicknesses. They keep the fabric taut while stitching, and are essential for fine work on thin fabrics. Hand-held oval and round hoops may be used for small projects and for carrying the needlework with you. Clamp-on, sit-on models and floor-standing square and oval hoops provide a larger working surface and leave both hands free for stitching. Artist's stretcher frame moldings up to about twenty-four inches long can be used if one wants to tack or staple the fabric to the frame. Larger sizes tend to warp.

Hoops are designed so the material can be moved about in them. Delicate materials and raised stitching can be damaged by the pressure of a hoop, so place tissue paper over the fabric before pushing the hoops together, then tear away the tissue from the sewing area. Remove the hoops before putting the work aside to prevent creasing the material.

You can work without a frame on thick fabrics and on needlework canvas. However, long Satin Stitches and Chain Stitches tend to be uneven and pucker when worked without a frame.

TRANSFERRING PATTERNS AND DESIGNS

Modern sewing counters offer several devices for marking dress patterns and needlework designs. Different fabrics will require different methods; always experiment to discover the best procedure for a given material.

Tracing and Carbon Transfers

For sheer fabrics, a design sketched on tracing or other paper can be placed beneath the taut material and traced onto the fabric with tailor's chalk or a pencil.

For opaque fabrics use dressmaker's carbon available in colors; select one close to your fabric color. (Do not use office carbon paper.) Trace your design onto ordinary tracing paper. Position and pin the design onto the fabric. Slip the carbon between the fabric and the design with the waxed side of the carbon next to the fabric, and trace over the design lines with a sharp pencil, stylus, or tracing wheel. Remove the pins and carbon and you may want to go over the design with a thin basting thread.

Hot Iron Transfer Pencils

Transferring a convenient preprinted design to fabric can be easily accomplished with your own designs by using a hot iron transfer pencil available in craft and needlework shops.

Place the traced drawing facedown on a hard surface and go over the lines from the *back* with the hot iron transfer pencil. Place the back side with the transfer pencil on it down on the fabric and press slowly with an iron heated to the temperature required for the fabric. Lift a corner to check for adequate transfer. (Follow directions for individual pencil brands.)

Thread Tracing

Where the above methods are impractical, you can "thread trace" with a procedure similar to basting. Place the design traced on tissue paper onto your fabric and pin or baste in place. Outline the design with running stitches made through both the paper and fabric. Then pull the tissue away from both sides of the thread line. When the project is completed, pull out the thread tracing.

NOTE: Positioning and transferring designs to clothing requires careful planning. When a motif is used on both halves of a garment, one side must be transferred with the design reversed, or "flopped," so it will match on both sides of the garment. Generally, motifs should be positioned so they do not extend into seam allowances or be caught up in darts that will distort them. Some embroidery is more easily done before the garment parts are assembled; others, afterward.

Altering the Size of the Design

Designs may be used in the sizes they appear in the patterns or taken directly from printed source books. In many instances you will wish to reduce or enlarge a design using the method shown at right. Also feel free to straighten a design, or to fragment and rearrange the parts and combine them in a new arrangement suitable for your purpose. For altering designs you will need tracing paper, graph or square paper, a ruler, a fine felt-tipped pen, a soft pencil, an eraser, and carbon paper (office variety for this procedure). The original drawing can be keyed with colored pencils or markers for color placement on the fabric.

IRONING, BLOCKING

Ironing is essential for finished clothing. The embroidery work may require special attention with a steam iron. It should be pressed from the back on a thickly padded surface such as several layers of terry toweling. This is essential to prevent beaded work, trapunto, and heavily embroidered areas from flattening. When a background has been badly stretched out of shape, place the padding on a board large enough to accommodate the entire piece of work. Stretch the fabric and pin it to the padding with the stitching side up. Square off as necessary with a ruler or T square. Sponge the embroidery carefully with warm water and allow to dry for twenty-four hours. When dry, turn over and press with steam iron if necessary.

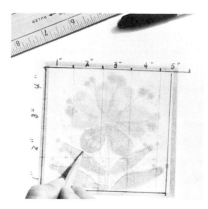

ENLARGING, REDUCING
You will need tracing paper, carbon, ruler, and pencil or marker. In the illustration, a 4-square-inch design is being enlarged to 6 square inches. Sketch the outline of the picture on a piece of tracing paper that has been squared off and divided into 1-inch squares.

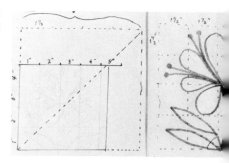

Draw a diagonal line through the sketch from the lower left corner extending to the upper right corner as shown. Measure off a 6-inch square and divide into 1½-inch squares. Draw a general reproduction of the small image in the enlargement, using the lines in each individual square as your guide for placement.

Trace the enlarged design onto your 6-inch fabric with a sheet of tracing paper. To make large designs smaller, reduce the size of the squares.

BASIC STITCHES AND THEIR APPEARANCE

FLAT STITCHES

Embroidery stitches develop logically from one another. The basic stitch vocabulary that follows begins with flat stitches that are easy to do and are essential for forming lines and outlining. When used imaginatively with varied colors and textures of threads, they can form infinitely exciting patterns.

Embroidery stitches are the foundation of the majority of surface embellishments on the clothing and accessories of many cultures. Appliqué, patchwork, quilting, needlepoint, crewel, and so forth are variations of embroidery stitches. Stitches are easily divided into categories: flat, crossed over flat, looped, chain, and knotted, with infinite combinations.

The designs shown with several stitches are offered as instantly usable samplers. Work the designs directly onto a garment and accomplish two things at once. If you are timid about your stitching ability, work the sampler on a separate piece of fabric; when it is perfect, appliqué it onto a clothing article or other item for an exotic detail.

Additional stitches and variations are offered in subsequent chapters with suggestions for their application.

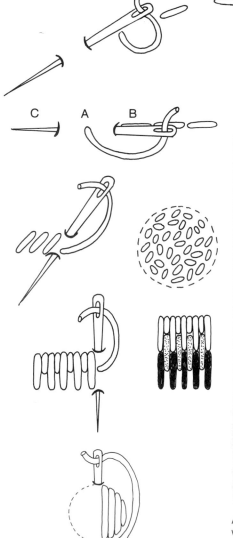

Running Stitch. Stitches of an even length are evenly spaced along a straight or curved line.

Backstitch. Bring the needle up from the back to the top of the fabric at A. Make a small stitch backward, placing the needle through the cloth at B; bring the tip a little in front of the first stitch at C. All stitches should be the same length.

Straight Stitch. Stitches of any length in any direction.
The **Seed Stitch** is composed of short straight stitches.

Long and Short Stitch. Different progressions of the Straight Stitch are used for shading and for filling. Alternating long and short stitches yields an appealing broken line for flowers and other solid areas.

Satin Stitch. Used for filling solid areas; it consists of Straight Stitches worked close together. To save thread a "surface" Satin Stitch can be done. Rather than bring your needle behind the fabric, bring it up very close and next to the previous stitch so the thread does not fill in the back of the cloth. Additional Satin Stitches are shown on page 28.

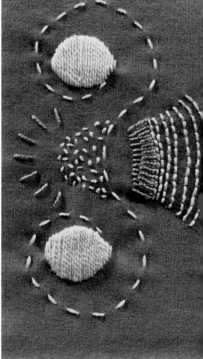

A design, loosely derived from a Malagan wood bas-relief from New Ireland, Oceania, was interpreted for the sampler using only the stitches on this page. Worked by Mandy Arrington.

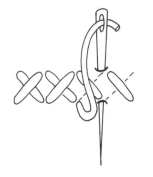

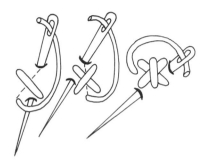

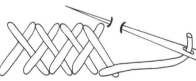

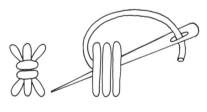

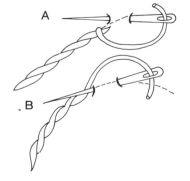

FLAT CROSS-OVER STITCHES

Cross Stitch. Generally, rows of Cross Stitches are made in a regular sequence with one leg of the stitch slanted and taken first and the other leg worked across it at the center for a neat appearance. For variety, the Cross Stitch may be worked individually in any direction and with legs uneven. (Also see "Counted Cross Stitching"—page 40.)

Star Stitch. A variation of the Cross Stitch. After the two threads are crossed, a third thread is worked vertically over the first two. These legs may also be varied in length, and in the number of stitches that cross to appear as "stars" with even or uneven points. All Cross-over Stitches also may be used to "couch" or hold down other threads.

Herringbone. Also referred to as a long-legged Cross Stitch. Work the stitches along lightly pencil-marked, or imaginary, guidelines. Both the top and bottom of each leg cross one another. For variety, change sizes of stitches and combine different weights and textures of threads on alternating legs.

Closed Herringbone. Differs from the above in that the tips of the stitches touch; the needle comes out through the same hole as that made by the previous stitch. It is used for narrow or wide borders and can be varied by the angle of the stitch. It is also called the Double Back Stitch, because a double row of Back Stitches results on the underside.

Sheaf Stitch. Used in groups for filling and in rows for borders in horizontal or vertical positions. Work three vertical straight stitches of equal length with even spaces between them. Bring your needle up alongside the first stitch slightly above center. Pass the needle over all the stitches and bring it under them *without picking up fabric.* Gently draw them together to make the first wrap. Make a second wrap the same way. Insert the needle into the fabric to the right of the last stitch and proceed to the next series of verticals.

Stem Stitch. Used for outlining, for flower stems, and for filling. The appearance differs when the thread is held under or over the needle. a) *Thread under the needle* on all stitches. Insert the needle on a slant half the length of the stitch and place your thumb on the resulting loop of thread. b) When the *thread* is placed *over the needle* on all stitches the appearance changes. Try adjacent rows of alternating under-the-needle and over-the-needle stitching for eye-appealing variations.

Designs based on a headpiece detail from figures on an ancient Mexican manuscript, *The Codex Nuttall,* are developed using the stitches illustrated on this page. Worked by Mandy Arrington.

LOOPED STITCHES

All *flat stitches* are considered "straight" stitches because the thread is carried straight from one point to another. When the thread is altered from its straight line by pulling it to one side with the needle or another thread, it is considered a *looped stitch*. The basis of the looped stitch is the Buttonhole Stitch, which can be worked in different directions and sizes or alternations of stitches and spaces between them, by placing one stitch on top of another, by one-half and three-quarter overlaps, and more.

Buttonhole or Blanket Stitch. The basic looped stitch is used for edging, outlining, and filling. Whether it is worked in a circle or straight, the procedure is the same. Bring the needle up at A, hold the thread down with your thumb. Bring the needle and thread around to the right, insert the needle at B and *bring the point out* at C, over the loop and in line with A.

Long and Short Buttonhole is one of hundreds of possible variations. Alternate the length of the stitch, and also the distance between the stitches as desired. Also try two stitches next to each other before inserting the needle at C.

Closed Buttonhole Stitches are made in pairs that form triangles. Bring the thread up and through at A. Insert needle at B and hold the thread down below the needle. Bring the needle up through at C with the thread under the needle and pull through. Insert the needle again at B, hold the thread down and bring the needle up and through at D with the thread under.

Knotted Buttonhole has a knot at the end of each stitch. It makes interesting edges in even and in short and long stitches. Begin the stitch and make a loop from right to left over your left thumb and place the loop over the needle at point A. With the loop still around the needle, stitch into the fabric at B and bring the point out at C over the lower thread. Before drawing the needle through, tighten the loop around the needle by pulling on the working thread.

Padded Buttonhole yields a raised effect when it is worked over a series of Running Stitches or Straight Stitches laid onto the work previously. For color variation, the under stitches can be one color and the Buttonhole another and the under color allowed to show through.

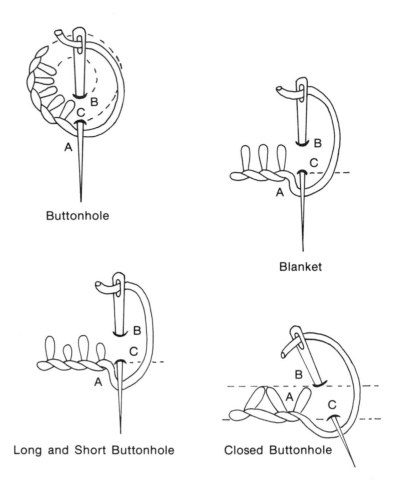

Buttonhole

Blanket

Long and Short Buttonhole

Closed Buttonhole

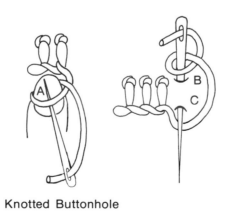

Knotted Buttonhole

Padded Buttonhole

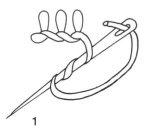

1   2

Buttonhole with Picot

Buttonhole with Picot. A picot is a small ornamental detail that forms an extra edging along the bottom of the Buttonhole Stitch. Work the plain Buttonhole Stitch until a picot is desired. 1) Hold the horizontal thread down with the left hand and twist the thread three times around the needle. Hold the thread securely and pull the working thread until the twisted threads are close to the stitch. 2) Make the Buttonhole Stitch into the last loop. Continue making basic Buttonhole Stitches until the next picot is desired.

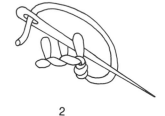

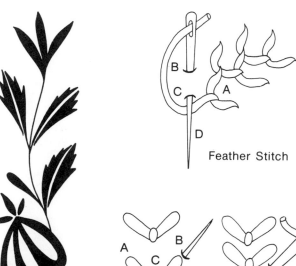

Looped Stitch

Looped Stitch yields a texture that looks like a centipede and is often referred to as a "Centipede" Stitch. Work from right to left. Bring the thread up at A, down at B, and up at C. Hold the thread with your thumb above C and bring the needle under the stitch, as shown; over D with the needle point over the thread. Begin the next stitch at E keeping the "spine" of the row evenly placed.

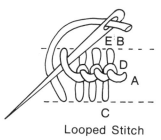

Feather Stitch

Feather Stitch. A series of Buttonhole Stitches worked on a line but made alternately from one side to the other. Bring the thread out at A; hold the thread with the thumb and bring the needle in at B and to the side of A. Bring the point out at C on top of the thread and pull through. For the next stitch, place the needle at D on the alternate side of the imaginary "line." To anchor the last stitch, place a small stitch next to the loop. Feather Stitches can be made with innumerable variations: single, double, triple, slanted, interlaced, as a couching, overlapping, and so forth.

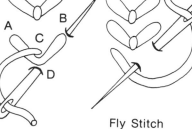

Fly Stitch

Fly Stitch, also called the Y Stitch, is simple to do and fun to vary. The uprights of the "Y" can be made longer and close or far apart. Bring your thread up at A and hold it down with your left thumb. Insert your needle at B and bring it up at C. Pull through and insert it below the loop at D to attach it. Position it below A where desired for the beginning of the next stitch. The length of the loop held with your thumb and the distance of the thread from A to B determine the size of the stitch.

Left:
Floral designs are basic to many cultures and can be interpreted with a variety of Buttonhole Stitches. Here is one possible pattern. Experiment with others and make up your own combinations, using all the stitches possible so you learn how to do them.

CHAIN STITCHES

A Chain Stitch is essentially a closed loop of the Buttonhole Stitch. When the needle that forms the loop of the Buttonhole Stitch is inserted into the fabric at about the same place it emerges, a Chain Stitch results. Chain Stitches may be used for line and fill; they are quick to work, and make attractive motifs. More Chain Stitches are illustrated on page 29.

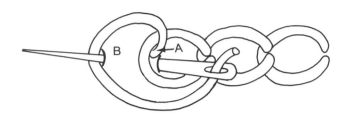

Basic Chain

Basic Chain Stitch is made by bringing the thread out at A and holding a loop of desired size down with the thumb. Insert the needle back next to point A and bring the point out a short distance away at B with the *thread under* the needle. Pull and the thread is ready for point A of the next stitch.

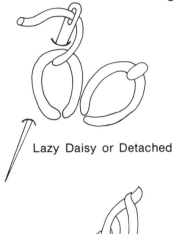

Lazy Daisy or Detached Chain Stitch. Work the same way as the Chain Stitch, above, but fasten each loop by bringing a small stitch over the top of the chain. Always hold the loop with your thumb. The stitch may be formed individually and in groups for flower petals.

Lazy Daisy or Detached

Twisted Chain. Begin by bringing the thread through at A as in the basic Chain, but instead of inserting the needle back next to A, place it slightly to the left of the last stitch at B. Hold the loop with your thumb and make a small slanting stitch and bring the needle up on the line of the design with the loop under the needle. Pull the thread through. For best effects, the loops should be worked close together.

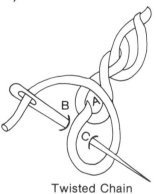

Twisted Chain

Open Chain Stitch is illustrated along two parallel lines, but it can vary in width from a narrow to a wide span. Bring the thread up at A. Hold a loop down with your left thumb and insert the needle at B. Bring the needle up at C with the loop under the needle. Insert the needle at D and, with the thread held under the needle point, allow another loop for the next stitch and bring the needle up at new point A.

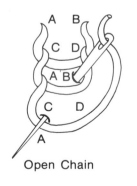

Open Chain

A Coptic design could be worked as a border or a single panel using Twisted Chains, French Knots, Bullion, and other stitches.

Checkered or Magic Chain is worked with two threads of different colors. The threads alternate for each loop. Place two colors of thread in your needle and work in the same way as the Basic Chain. Bring both threads up at A. Loop and hold *only one color* under your thumb for the first stitch. Note that one color is placed under the needle point and the other over it. Bring both threads back down next to A and pull through and up at B. On the next stitch, switch threads.

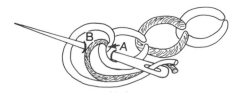

Checkered or Magic

18

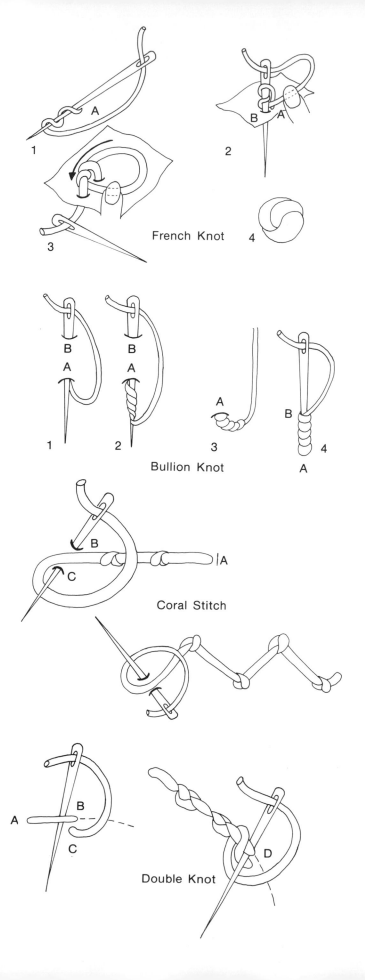

French Knot

Bullion Knot

Coral Stitch

Double Knot

KNOTTED STITCHES

Knotted Stitches form textural and visual "knobs," or raised effects, on the fabric. The French and Bullion knots are worked as detached stitches; others are worked along the thread and attached to the fabric. All of them may be used for linear designs, for fill, and for accents in any direction.

French Knot is a detached stitch made by winding the thread around the needle. Work on fabric in a hoop. 1) Bring thread to top at A. Wind the needle with the thread one, two, or three times holding the winding thread taut. 2) Push the needle down and through the fabric at B, which is *close to A* but *not* in the same hole, and continue holding the thread taut. 3) It will look like this as the knot begins to form but you must keep the top thread taut or it will all unwind. 4) The finished knot.

Bullion Knot looks like the back of a tiny armadillo and can be made in many lengths. Work with the fabric taut. 1) Bring thread up at A and insert needle at B. This will be the distance you want the Bullion Knot to be. Bring the needle from the back of the fabric up through A again but do not pull through. Let the needle shank protrude. 2) Wind the thread around the needle shank as many times as it takes to equal the distance between A and B. 3) Carefully pull the needle through the fabric and all the loops. 4) Secure the knot by pushing the needle down through at B.

Coral Stitch creates a textural interest in straight, curved, and zigzag borders. Bring the thread up at A, hold a loop with your thumb. Insert the needle through the fabric a distance from each knot at B and on a slight slant and with the thread under the needle tip. Pull through at C.

Double Knot Stitch is larger and more impressive than the Coral Stitch and may be used in conjunction with it to increase the appearance of a dimensional line. Take a stitch from A to B and bring the needle up through the fabric at C. Place the needle under the thread only (not through the fabric). With the thread under the needle, pass the needle again under the first stitch at D. Pull the thread through to form a knot. Space the knots evenly and closely for a beaded effect, farther apart for a rhythmic border design.

COMBINATION STITCHES

Countless variations can be created by combining stitches and portions of them with other stitches. The following are frequently found on ethnic embroidery. More are illustrated throughout the book. Use them inventively as you plan your original designs from a variety of inspirations.

Couching is the practice of attaching long threads to the fabric surface with shorter holding stitches. Lay one or multiple threads along the design line and take small stitches at regular intervals with another thread. Placement, angle, color, and size of couched and holding threads add to the possible variety.

Closed Couching. Stitches that hold the couched threads are placed close to each other over another thread to form a raised line often called Overcast or Trailing Stitch. Threads also may be couched with groups of two Straight Stitches, with Cross, Buttonhole, Herringbone, Fly, Feather, Open Chains, and any other stitches that you like to work with. Threads to be couched may be held in place with pins or masking tape until they are attached.

Split Stitch actually splits the thread to create the design for flat-fill areas in a delicate motif. Bring the thread up at A. The length of the stitch is determined by the placement of the needle at B and C. Insert the needle into the fabric at B and bring it up at C splitting the thread with your needle as you come up.

PILE STITCHES

Pile Stitches are the same as those used with thick yarns in heavy backing for making rugs and referred to as Ghiordes and Rya knots. They can be made with needle and thread on embroidery fabric with thin or thick yarns for a pile effect, called "Turkey work."

1. Bring thread up at A. Hold the yarn *above* the needle; go down at B, up at C (halfway between AB). Pull through snugly.
2. With the yarn *below* the needle, go down at D, up at B (DB should equal CB). Pull, and leave a loop.
3. With the yarn *above* the needle, go down at E, up at D. Pull the thread through snugly.
4. With the yarn *below* the needle, go down at F, up at E, and leave a loop. Continue alternating the yarn *above* the needle for the flat holding stitches and *below* the needle for the loops, keeping the loops even.
5. A row of finished loops.
6. The loops may be cut to result in a cut, or shaggy, pile.

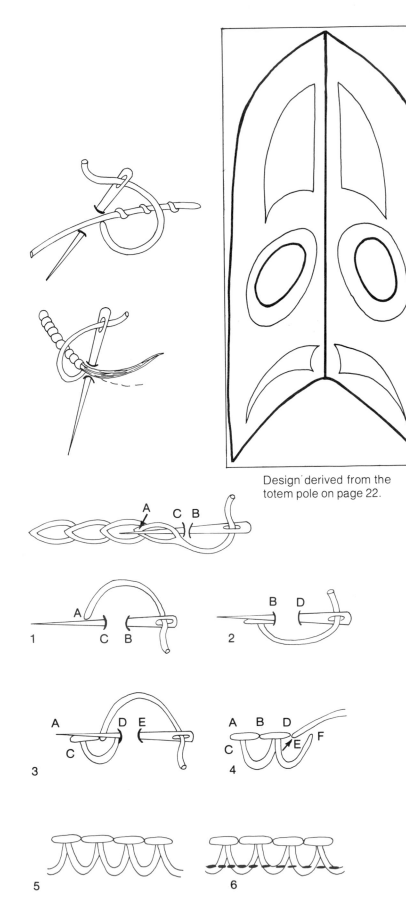

Design derived from the totem pole on page 22.

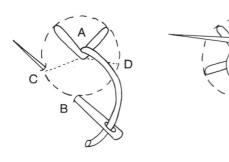

Border designs are effective with these stitches; the progression for linear and round designs can be developed for cuffs and trim on countless garments; above was inspired by the Mexican mask on page 22 (*bottom left*).

LACED OR THREADED STITCHES

Threaded Stitch is very effective when accomplished with threads of different colors and textures, and with different progressions.

Double-Threaded Running Stitch is worked with two needles and the stitches are laced the same way shoes are laced. Only the running stitches show on the back; the lacings are held to the fabric by the running stitch.

Pekinese Stitch consists of a line of Back Stitches used as a foundation for loops. The loops are shown open but they should be pulled slightly. For looping, bring your needle up through the fabric at A—then all work is done *without piercing* the material. Take your needle up and under stitch 2, down and under 1 with the point on top of the loop. Then up under 3, down and under 2, and so forth.

Spider-Web Stitch begins with a Fly Stitch. Mark a circle with a coin or a compass. Make a Fly Stitch with the point at the circle center A and carry the stitch to bottom of center B. Make two additional stitches between C and A, A and D, so the circle is divided into five equal sections. Bring the thread up under one spoke and begin to weave over one, under one, around in a circle. Some of the spoke thread will show. Weaving can be accomplished with threads colored the same or different from the spokes.

Wrapped Variation. To cover all the spokes, wrap each spoke with the thread, as shown. A raised circular effect will result.

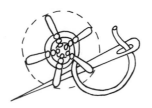

A model totem pole of the Northwest Coast Indians has several eye shapes and outlines that you might use in other contexts. The shape itself could suggest a small doll form or a mask.

Photographed at
San Diego Museum of Man

A painted papier-mâché skull from Mexico has brilliantly painted flowers with simple shapes and scrolls that could be adapted to embroidery, beading, appliqué and more.

A Guatemalan woman's woven and embroidered garments exhibit flowers not unlike those in the Mexican mask above. The woven designs are symbols of the culture, but the automobiles on the basket cover are the Guatemalan interpretation of modern technology.

COLOR, TEXTURE

Ethnic clothing is frequently a kaleidoscope of color. Vivid, bright, romantic colors often reflect the climate of the country of origin. Mexican embroideries are sensuous and gay, with multiple contrasting colors and radiant shading. Stitcheries from such northern countries as Norway and Sweden tend to be more subdued, less flamboyant than those from the Mediterranean areas. And because much of the work is done by people without formal art training, the schemes do not necessarily follow any rigid rules of contrast and complementary colors.

The more appealing designs, however, usually adhere to certain elements that suggest innate good taste. No matter how many patterns and colors are used, some elements always seem to predominate—and that is a good simple rule for you to follow. You can alter the shading and toning of a dominant color in different amounts, then add the other colors in lesser amounts. Think of your threads as paint on a palette; lay them next to each other on the fabric with which you intend to use them. If you like the combinations in the skeins and balls, you'll like them when they are worked into surface embellishments.

The choice is yours; select color schemes from any cultural source you like, mix them, match them, rearrange them. Use a cool color combination with designs from a wild exuberant culture; try flickering, gay colors with a design derived from someplace somber and cold. The entire mood of the piece will be altered. Add beads and mirrors, sequins and ribbons, too. Follow the dictates of your own taste as do the needleworkers in other countries and you will establish your own personal variety of folk art.

Textures are an important consideration of design. The threads and fabrics themselves have textures for you to work with, but you can consciously arrange textures around your work in the same way you

arrange color. You might want a piece entirely of silks that will shimmer and glisten like the figures on a Japanese kimono. Cotton threads or fibers may be more compatible to blue jean decoration. Combinations of shiny and dull, smooth and fuzzy, can add great visual interest to an area and to a very simple design.

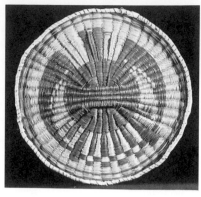

The Hopi Indians weave a tray with a bird design that could be copied for appliqué or embroidery on the back of a blouse.
*Photographed at
San Diego Museum of Man*

DESIGNS, IDEAS

Throughout the book, we stress sources for design in ethnic cultures. Several specific patterns are offered for you to apply in any creative way you like. In addition, train your eye to absorb details that can be developed into original needlework designs. You need not use an entire border copied exactly as you see it shown on another embroidery or on a printed fabric or an object. Use only a small detail of that design and explode it into a complete new motif.

Learn to look for ideas in objects other than needlework—the trim on a cloisonné dish, the details in a wood or stone carving from another culture. The zigzag around the eye of a painted African mask can be the exact border you need for a cuff or a collar in a progression of Cross Stitches that may not have occurred to you.

Figures can be as intricate or as simplified as you like. Try using figures from jewelry, stylized birds and animal shapes from Indian baskets, and drawings from the ancient caves in France.

There are countless books and magazines with photos in color that can spark your creative thoughts along exotic lines. In the same photos, discover ideas for ciothing patterns, methods for wrapping scarves, and combinations of patterns and accessories that will make you, your wardrobe, and your accessories sparkle in a crowd.

Detail of a mythical garuda bird from Bali offers excellent embroidery design details.
Collection, Diane Powers

A silver necklace from Afghanistan has tiny figures and detailing ideal for padded embroidery and trapunto designs.
*Photographed at The Bazaar
del Mundo, San Diego*

The Rio Grande Pueblo Indians of New Mexico offer stylized geometric shapes with straight and curved motifs on a painted wooden drum.
*Photographed at
San Diego Museum of Man*

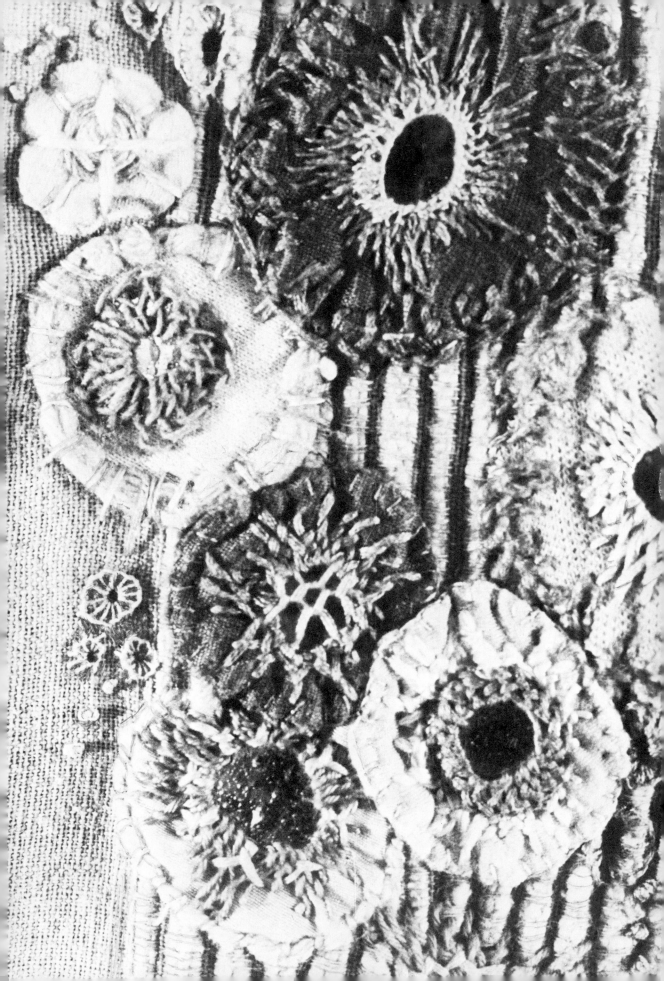

A jewel-bright embroidered sleeve adds
the individual touch to a handmade dress
with ethnic styling by Nan Ferrin (detail
on page 24).

SATIN-STITCH VARIATIONS

The basic stitches in the previous chapters have myriad variations. They are easy to do and give stunning results. The embellishment ideas that follow may be copied or developed in your own individualized style with any stitch combinations.

Slanted Satin Stitch shown is the "surface" stitch mentioned on page 14. The thread is inserted through the fabric at top and bottom.

Padded Satin Stitch yields a raised and padded look and may consist of two or more layers to make the stitch higher and rounder. Lay one row of Satin Stitches in the desired shape in one direction; cover in the opposite, or a slanted, direction, keeping the edge lines neat as you stitch.

Fishbone Stitch begins with Running Stitches from the center of the shape to the tip. 1) Bring the needle up at A, insert at B and C on a slant so the resulting stitch lies to the left side of the center stitches. 2) Insert needle at D to the left of the center stitches and bring up at E so the stitch slants in the opposite direction and crosses. The needle is always worked from the center to the outer edge. For an Open Fishbone Stitch, space the slanted stitches to look like open "ribs."

Raised Fishbone Stitch. Start with the Running Stitch, as above. Make a deep Cross Stitch, as shown, with your needle emerging at A. Insert the needle horizontally at B and up at C, over and in at D, then horizontally to E. Continue to cross over—always placing the needle horizontally on the margins, below the leg of the previous crosses.

Roumanian Stitch, also called the Roman Stitch, is used by many European embroiderers for a textured fill stitch in broad areas. It is actually a long Flat Stitch held with a slanted Couching Stitch across the center. It can be worked from the top down or the bottom up. 1) Bring the thread out at A and over to B. Bring the needle up at C and slightly to the right of center and below the AB line with the thread under the needle point, as shown. 2) Insert the needle at D to make a slanted, small Couching Stitch and bring up at E to begin the next long Flat Stitch.

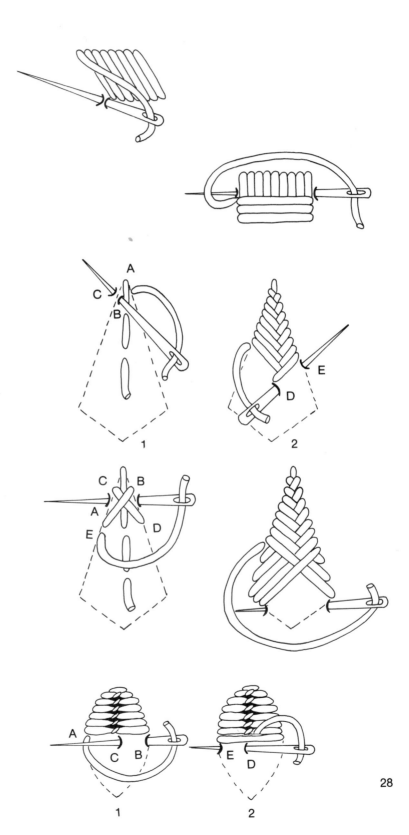

28

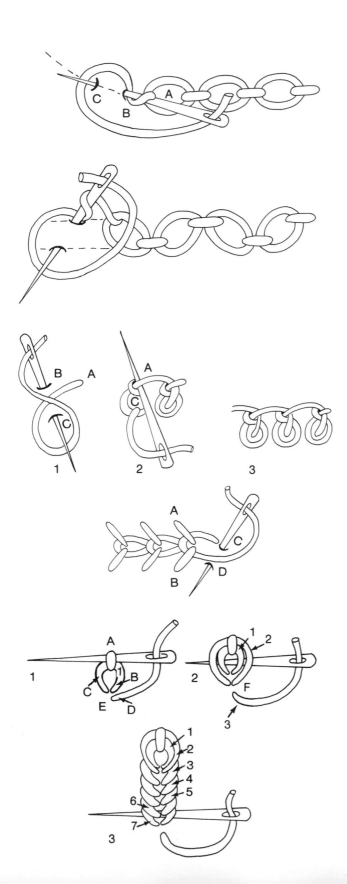

CHAIN-STITCH VARIATIONS

The basic Chain Stitch fills space quickly; the variations add interest to the finished embroidery.

Cable Chain Stitch creates a link between each loop. Bring the needle up at A. Hold the thread taut with your free hand and pass the thread over the needle shank from the top and around. Pull the thread up and hold it with your thumb to make the loop of the chain. Insert the needle below the wind at B and bring out at C with the point on top of the thread. The loop and/or the link can vary in length.

Zigzag Cable Chain offers more variety for linear decorations in assorted yarns along borders and for interior bands. Work the same as above, but alter the placement of the link and the loop at the top and bottom of a design line.

Rosette Chain Stitch is for decorative circular shapes and borders. Work from right to left. 1) Bring the thread up at A. Hold a loop slightly to the left of A with your other thumb. Insert your needle at B and come up on a slight angle at C with the loop under the needle. 2) Bring the thread under A from the bottom up and without entering the fabric and around to the left. 3) Finished example. Do the stitch slowly and place it carefully or it loses its shape. It requires a firm, heavy thread rather than a fine, silky-finish thread.

Wheat-Ear Chain Stitch. Work two Straight Stitches at A and B. Lace the thread under these stitches without entering the fabric. Insert your needle through the fabric at C and bring up and through at D.

Heavy Chain Stitch. Work from the top down. 1) To begin, take a small vertical stitch at A. Bring your needle up at B and lace it through the vertical stitch for chain 1 and go down at C. Reenter the fabric at D and lace the thread through the vertical stitch again and reenter the fabric at E. 2) Bring the needle out at F to make chain. 3) Follow the same procedure for all subsequent chains *except* always insert the needle under the last two chains made, as shown.

COMBINING STITCHES

Combinations of only a few stitches repeated in different sizes, colors, textures, and density can result in complex-appearing patterns.

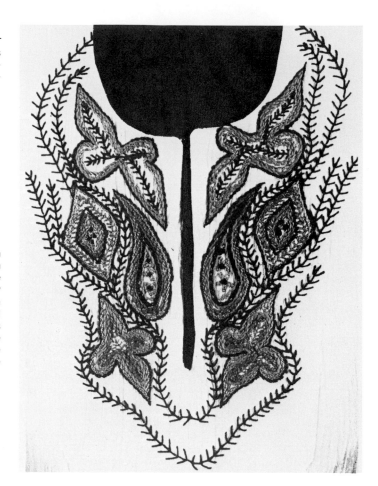

Carol Emerick used mainly the Fly Stitch with some Back Stitching and French Knots for an embroidered design she applied to the blouse front. The black Fly Stitching enclosed the shapes, which were isolated from portions of an Oriental rug. The purple and red scheme was suggested by the original rug. Use the drawing at right and enlarge for a blouse front or back; carry the Fly Stitch onto the cuff for added detailing.

A border design suggested by a Moroccan scarf can be made of Slanted Satin Stitches on each side of a row of Back Stitches and might be applied to pocket edges.

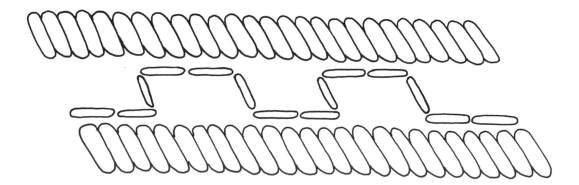

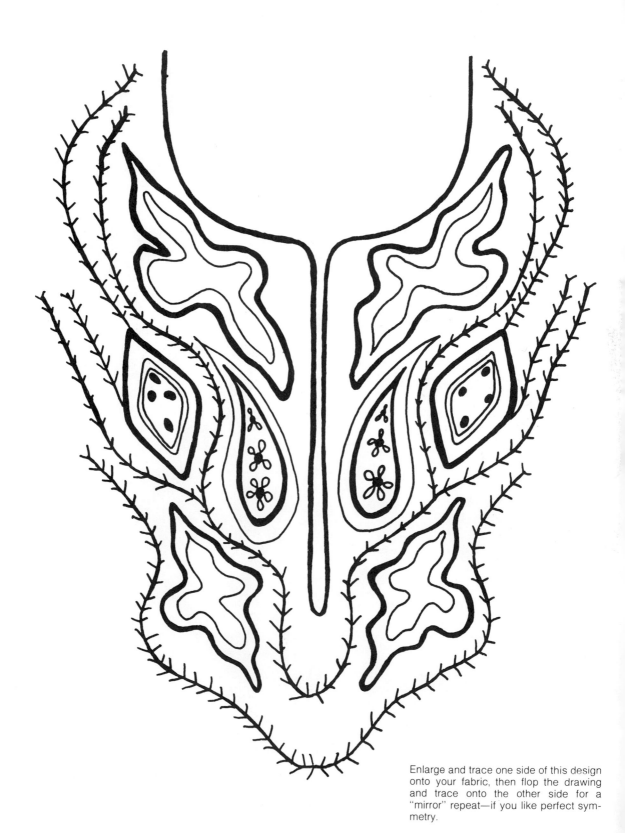

Enlarge and trace one side of this design onto your fabric, then flop the drawing and trace onto the other side for a "mirror" repeat—if you like perfect symmetry.

Opposite page and left:
Elisabeth Schimitschek used a Northwest Coast Indian printed fabric and added embroidery details with Chain Stitching. She created an original motif on the yoke with Satin Stitching, Back Stitching, and Twisted Chain Stitching.

Try enlarging individual motifs from other Indian cultures from the drawings shown. Repeat, overlap them, or combine them in appliqué with embroidery or in all-embroidery stitches for clothing and accessories.

An Afghanistan nomad dress, full-skirted and ankle length with a high-waisted bodice, is made from Folkwear Pattern 107. Shown are only three of countless ways it can be changed.

An embroidered panel with shi sha mirrors and beaded fringe is used for the bodice front. A floral print fabric at the top sleeve is combined with a solid color material at the sleeve bottom and for the shirt.

The same pattern is made with a dominantly Satin Stitch top, silver medallions, a beaded rondelle, and looped fringe. Velvet and flower print silk fabrics, culled from old garments, are pieced together to make the sleeves; the skirt is also velvet.

Drawings below are details that appear in the Folkwear pattern and are repeated in the top dress.

Courtesy, Folkwear
Photos, Jerry Wainright

Janet Martini interpreted the Afghanistan nomad dress pattern in several bold prints. A reverse-appliqué mola with ribbon and stitching around it is the front panel. Wide ribbons with hand embroidery border the sleeves. The skirt front has been revised with one panel rather than two.

The Thunderbird design (*far right*), painted on a drumhead by the Tsimshian (Northwest Coast) Indians, inspired the embroidery on a velveteen vest. The entire bird was used for the back, using mainly flat and padded Satin Stitches. Elements around the outer edge were picked up for the vest front with the bird design interpreted in a stylized manner on one side. By Berrylynn Freeby.

Diane Garick Mergenov translates thirteenth-century Serbian icons into surface-designed wall hangings using mainly Chain and Satin Stitches—thousands of them, in subtle shade gradations. She interprets the originals with threads as a painter or mosaicist would use pigments or tesserae.

A detail from the Byzantine mosaic "Empress Theodora and Attendants" at San Vitale, Ravenna (ca. 547, A.D.), could be interpreted as an entire stitched wall hanging; details could be developed for clothing embellishments. The entire mosaic, which may be found reproduced in color in art history books, could be a constant source for images, embroidery details, color combinations, and use of gold threads.

Courtesy, Alinari, Italy

"Saint George and the Dragon." Diane Garick Mergenov. 60 inches high, 40 inches wide.

Detail, Counted Thread Cross Stitching

COUNTED THREAD CROSS STITCHING

A basic Cross Stitch introduced in Chapter 2 can be embroidered on any fabric in loose arrangements and with variations in the sizes of the stitches. Another procedure is to work the Cross Stitch very evenly and in a planned order on a fabric with a pronounced warp and weft so that the threads can be counted. This method is referred to as "Counted Thread Cross Stitching."

Counted thread work is one of the most widely known international stitchery methods. Examples appear in national clothing throughout Europe, the Near East, and the Orient. It is particularly well adapted to geometric patterns. Counted Thread Cross Stitch designs may be used both by themselves and in conjunction with other stitches to interpret ethnic designs authentically, or to transpose the mood of one culture into a statement of another. For example: a Japanese border design can be plotted in Cross Stitch onto the bib of a Roumanian blouse pattern. A Pennsylvania Dutch painted tray pattern can be captured as Cross Stitching on linen or other fabric.

Almost any kind of thread from fine silk floss and pearl cotton to crewel and tapestry yarns can be used effectively for the geometric Cross Stitching. Linen, huck toweling, and fine canvas are good ground fabrics to begin with.

Do not use an embroidery hoop; it tends to stretch the fabric, and the stitches become loose when the material is removed. Work small pieces in your hands; large pieces can be worked on a needlepoint frame. Always keep your threads from twisting by allowing the needle and thread to hang free; unwind the threads when they do twist.

There are two types of Cross Stitch design—positive and negative. In positive designs, Cross Stitches are the pattern and the fabric is the background. In negative Cross Stitch, the background is filled in with the stitching. A traditional style, called Assisi work, is always done in two tones such as brown yarn on beige linen, an effective combination for contemporary work. The idea of a "limited palette" can be used in any tone-on-tone combination.

Working Suggestions

1. Plan your patterns on graph paper with each Cross Stitch in one square of the paper equaling a selected number of threads to be crossed over on the fabric.

2. Mark the center of the fabric and the center of the design. Run a basting thread through the fabric center and count the weave from the center outward. Note the number of threads to the inch.

3. Keep the fabric pulled and even as you work so the warp and weft can be easily counted, but do not use a hoop. To simplify counting threads on flat items such as linen place mats and panels that will be applied to something else, pull out one warp and one weft from each side of the material beyond the pattern. Then run a basting thread around the outer edge of the pattern placing a stitch at every inch of the weave so the fabric itself becomes a replica of the graph paper.

Needleworkers of the Meo Hill tribe of northern Thailand wear Cross-Stitched panels around their blouse necklines which they sew in a symbolic repeat motif they have been using for generations.

The precision of Counted Thread Cross Stitching can be observed in a Mexican overblouse in bright pinks and blues on white cotton. The angles and squares created by the stitching are repeated in the macramé borders. A Buttonhole Stitch trims the neckline.

4. Always cross the threads over in the same direction for pattern consistency. In large areas, embroider only one leg of the stitch, and in one direction only, all across the work (Half Cross Stitch), then complete the cross in the other direction. That way the upper stitch will always lie in the same direction. Stitches that are not placed consistently over one another catch light differently and appear to be mistakes. When working small areas, stitches can be made individually, taking care to keep the correct leg on the top to match larger fill areas.

When the warp and weft threads are distinct and can be counted, the legs of the Cross Stitch make an even square. When working, slant a row of "legs" in one direction. Then come back and make the second leg cross over so one thread will be consistently on top of the other in the same direction.

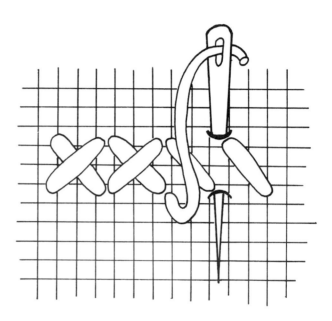

Cross Stitches completely fill the fabric and result in geometric designs of different colors. The inside design is separated from the border by three rows of Half Cross Stitches slanted in one direction.

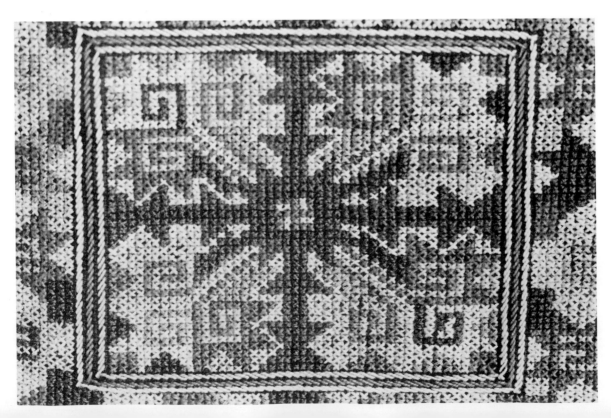

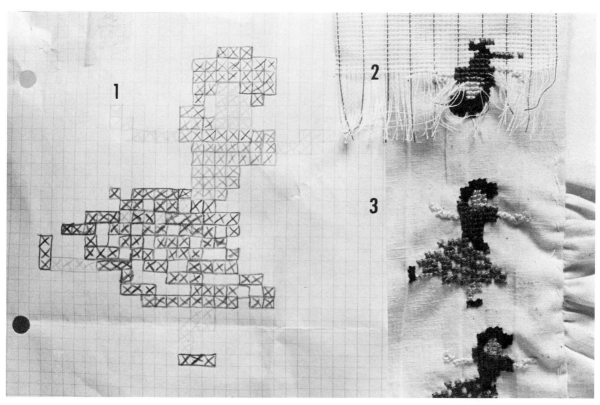

PULLED THREAD COUNTED CROSS STITCH METHOD

The geometry of Counted Thread work can be accomplished on fine or unevenly woven fabrics by using the technique shown here.

1. Plan the design on graph paper using different-colored pencils to represent the thread colors.

2. Baste a square of soft, open-mesh cotton canvas to the fabric. Sew the Cross Stitch pattern through the canvas and the base fabric but *do not pierce or split* any of the canvas threads in the stitching or pull the stitches too tight. When the embroidery is completed, gently pull the canvas threads out from under the Cross Stitching, one by one, alternating warp and weft threads as necessary (see detail below).

3. The finished stitched figure.

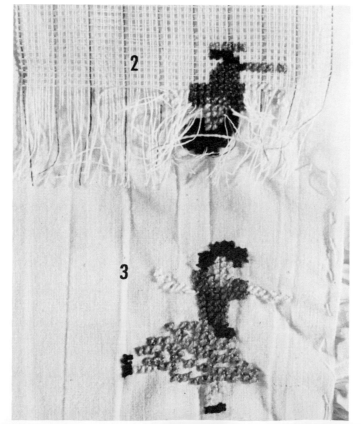

Detail of above. This same technique can be applied to portions of already assembled garments that are hard to flatten because of darts and seams. By Dusty Eisner.

A dress from Syria is heavily and intricately embroidered in red Cross Stitches on black wool. The design consists of a series of squares and triangles.

Collection, Mrs. Harriette Chandler, Chula Vista, California

Folkwear Pattern No. 105 offers the Syrian dress pattern with a simple Cross Stitch design developed from the more intricate original. Any segment may be used in a more or less complex repeat. The dress pattern could be altered and cut for a short dress, a tunic, or an overblouse.

The same Syrian dress could take on a completely different character embellished with designs divorced from the original. Try figures taken from a Russian peasant design motif.

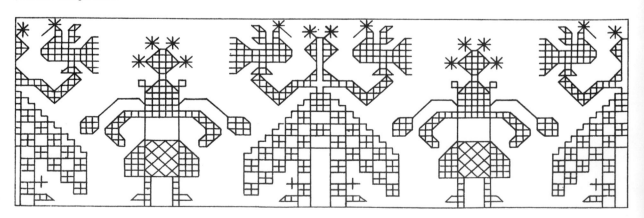

A youngster's Turkish tunic top is embroidered with black thread using a combination of Cross Stitches, Back Stitches, and Holbein Stitches. A counted-thread design in black thread on white is often referred to as "Blackwork," which possibly evolved from Arabic and Moorish examples in Spain. It reached a peak in Britain from 1500 to 1650, so is primarily thought of as Elizabethan.

Courtesy, Folkwear
Photo, Jerry Wainwright

SHI SHA MIRROR IDEAS

About the time that contemporary craftspeople began a new romance with needlework in the late 1960s, import shops displayed a stunning variety of items from India. Much of the beautiful, flamboyant Indian work had small embroidered mirrors on the surface. Within months, craft-shop suppliers scurried to discover and sometimes create sources for tiny round mirrors to supply the increasing demand. Where ¾-, 1-, and 2-inch-diameter mirrors were unheard of before, they are now stacked up on counters; they are enticing needleworkers to apply them in ingenious ways.

The shi sha mirror is evidently here to stay and no one would probably be less surprised at this than the Rabari women of the Kutch desert in India.[1] To them, embroidering is a way of life, and in their extremely hot, dry, monotonous climate, embroidery adds gaiety and color; embroidery threads strengthen otherwise short-lived fabrics. The actual embroidering becomes a social event, a chance for women and girls to come together and talk while making constructive use of their time. Embroidery appears in men's clothing and household items as well as in women's wear. Many of the designs are based on motifs and symbology that narrate the folklore and the way of Rabari life from the beginning of time to the present.

The Rabari use mainly square and triangular mica mirrors, while another group, the Sindhis, more commonly use round ones. Both the Rabari and Sindhis use strong cotton or silk thread with an interwoven stitch that holds the mirrors to the material. This is probably the first stitch emulated by contemporary needleworkers when the idea of adding mirrors to clothing, accessories, and wall hangings caught their attention. Since then, additional methods for attaching the mirrors have been developed and they are shown on the following pages.

Small mirrors are available from craft suppliers and are easy to find today. You can also use pieces of Mylar, silver plastic, and heavy foil depending upon the function of the fabric it will be attached to. Washability, cleanability, and so forth must be considered, as mirrors of glass may crack and break.

Placing mirrors within your own embroidery is one way to incorporate the shimmering lively look of Indian fabrics; another is to purchase an object embroidered in India, cut it apart and create something new by the addition of embroidery and appliqué and other needlework ideas offered throughout the book.

A "choli," or a festive blouse with square mirrors, indicates that it is probably from Rabari, India. The mirror decoration is only on the front panel and sleeves; the garment ties in the back and is worn over other garments on special occasions. *Collection, Mr. & Mrs. Wayne Chapman, Solana Beach, California*

[1] Judy Frater, "The Meaning of Folk Art in Rabari Life," *Textile Museum Journal,* vol. 4, no. 2 (Washington, D.C.: The Textile Museum, 1975), pp. 47–60.

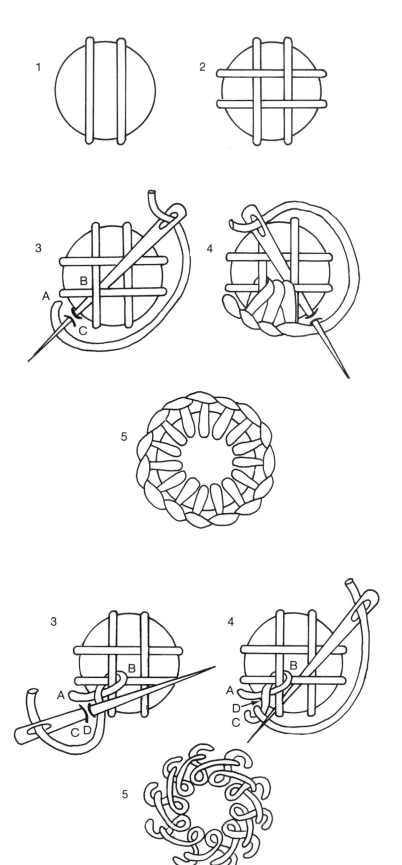

ATTACHING SHI SHA MIRRORS

Studying the needlework methods used by East Indian, Persian, and other Eastern cultures for attaching shi sha mirrors reveals variations in the stitches used—each yields a slightly different surface appearance. The stitches may also be used without the mirrors. French Knots or a bead may be used in the center for an attractive alternation. Basic Buttonhole and Cretan stitches usually attach and surround the mirror, with other stitches and additional rows of the same stitch overlapped. Knots may be intermixed with the edge of the stitch. Be as inventive as you like to enrich the surface decoration.

BUTTONHOLE STITCH SHI SHA ATTACHMENT

Hold the mirror on the fabric with the thumb and forefinger of one hand;

1. Stitch with the other hand and secure the mirror to the cloth with two vertical threads quite close together.

2. Take two horizontal threads and "weave" them under and over the vertical threads.

3. Bring your needle up at A. Place it under the intersecting spokes at B. Bring the needle through the fabric at C with the thread under the needle point.

4. Continue placing the threads under the spokes and space the inserted stitches evenly around the circumference of the mirror. The spokes will pull, so it is necessary to work carefully to result in a neat center.

5. The shi sha mirror attached (see next page).

CRETAN STITCH SHI SHA ATTACHMENT

Begin as in 1 and 2, above, for the spokes.

3. Bring the stitch up at A, around and under the spokes at B, cross over the thread. Insert your needle in the fabric at the mirror edge at C, up at D with the point over the thread.

4. Pass the needle under the spokes and over the thread. Continue as in 3.

5. The appearance is a circle of finished Cretan Stitches (see next page).

Opposite page:
A knitted fabric in a modernized version of a caftan by Twyla Cottrell is elegant in its simplicity. Yet the embellishments are detailed and delicate. Twyla appliquéd hand-crocheted doilies to the dress front. Inspired by the shi sha idea she added beads instead of mirrors.

A Buttonhole Stitch shi sha attachment.

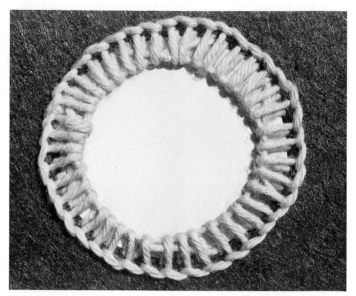

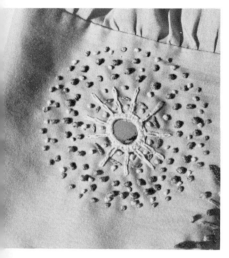

A Buttonhole Stitch shi sha decoration on a cuff with Chain Stitches, Running Stitches, and French Knots. By Dee Menagh.

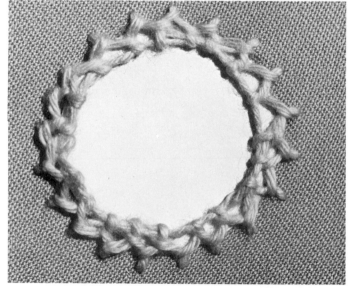

A Cretan Stitch shi sha attachment.

Several types of shi sha stitches and embroidery embellishments have been combined with mirrors, beading, and knots in the centers. By Nan Ferrin.

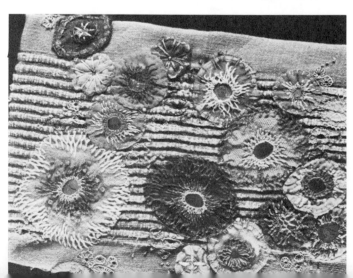

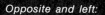

Opposite and left:
Panels of embroidered fabrics from India are so intricate and beautiful that you can use them to assemble onto other items that you make or buy. They are a quick trick for magically changing something ordinary into a smashingly exotic garment. A portion of an India hanging was cut and appliquéd to the front of a tunic. Careful utilization of the design revealed that it could easily be cut apart and positioned for the neckline; other cutout parts were hemmed and attached to the sleeve.

Collection, Mimi Levinson

Below:
An embroidered table runner was cut to fit around the back and the flap of a manufactured fabric purse. Additional Satin Stitching in triangles and rectangles was added along with beaded tassels. By B. J. Adams.

Embroidered panels from India with shi sha mirrors in various circular arrangements are made into a pillow cover. The joining bands are hand-embroidered to carry out the theme and colors. By Diane Powers.

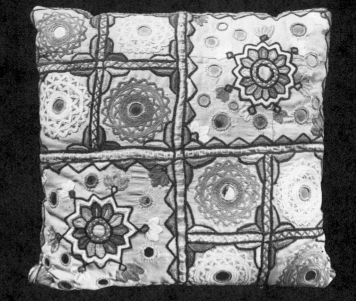

Boots made in India with Chain Stitch embroidery and shi sha mirrors.
Collection, Diane Powers

An opulently embroidered panel from India was fashioned as a box cover. A stuffed elephant and rider were perched on top. Pompons and ribbons were added at the corners, and a small pompon at the center front is used to lift the cover. By Diane Powers.

A panel with Star Stitching on the background and shi sha mirrors with petal shapes is used for a blouse front.

Hand-batiked fabric with embroidery and shi sha mirrors is appliquéd to the front of the dress on page 55. In this close-up detail you can observe the addition of beads. Chain Stitches are used in the flower petals with ribbon appliqué on the sides. By Nan Ferrin.

PUT IT ALL TOGETHER

This skirt by Frances Bardacke combines several techniques: Mirrors are stitched onto the appliquéd materials taken from lace and linen cutwork tablecloths. Cut-up upholstered pieces are worked into the design with squiggly free-style machine embroidery.

Opposite page:
Nan Ferrin creates a country-girl look with an elegant presentation through the combined use of appliqué and printed and embroidered panels thoughtfully developed into a cohesive entity. The back trim ends in a repeat pennant design.

Tony Prescott made a peasant-style blouse and crocheted medallions that she combined with hand embroidery. The back detail with tassels *(right)* illustrates how embroidery can create a yoke effect on a plain garment.

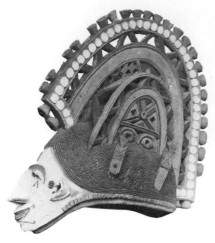

A carved headpiece from another culture can give you ideas for combining geometric shapes. Try circles within stripes, and triangles in a second row. The carved spirals are effective when translated into threads.
Courtesy, The British Museum, London

MORE IDEA SOURCES AND HOW TO APPLY THEM

Modern styling and mass production tend to result in restrained details on clothing. Every extra seam and stitching adds to the cost of producing the garment. Ideas for adding decorative detailing to ready-made clothes and to patterns for making your own clothes are as vast as the world itself. Once you learn where to look and how to focus in on details, you will be more concerned with selecting what you need than wondering where to find ideas.

You have been introduced to the world of exotic design in these early pages. Now you can begin to dig deeper, to see beyond the surface of a country's embroidery that you might emulate and adapt. You can begin to study not only their garments, but also their wall hangings, folk objects, pottery, paper cuttings, baskets, and woven textiles. You can pluck out bits and pieces that appeal to you just as you might select one petal from a flower. The following pages offer myriad suggestions for observing those bits, then interpreting and combining them into the needlework idiom.

Cross Stitching and flat fill-in stitches in intricate, yet symmetrical, geometric arrangements are associated with Middle Eastern countries. Try taking one band from this design and using it on a garment—perhaps around a skirt border or the front panel. It could be repeated in contrasting color combinations in a bolero or blouse; the blouse may be designed like the huipil at right and worn over a contemporary sweater.
Collection, Mr. & Mrs. Wayne Chapman, Solana Beach, California

Embroidered design for a shirt derived from a motif on a ceramic dish from Cyprus, Iron Age. By Alice Crowley.

Purse of assembled materials: needlepoint, beads, pompons, and tassels. By Diane Powers.

Byzantine mosaics were the inspiration for Diane Garick Mergenov's fabric mosaic intricately assembled skirt using many patterns suggested by folk wear.

Doll of mixed materials from Guatemala, India, and other countries with elaborate metal thread work, shi sha mirrors, coins, and hand embroidery. By Diane Powers.

A fabric mosaic jacket is based on early Roman Byzantine church designs. Cottons and velvets are all hand-stitched. By Diane Garick Mergenov.

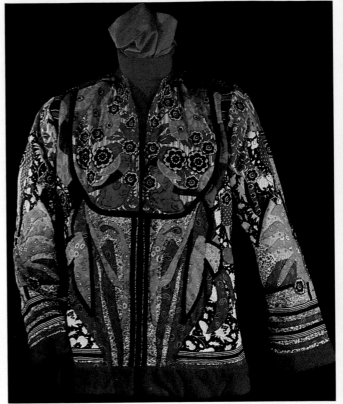

Log Cabin patchwork box based on an early American technique. Subtle coloring and a new use characterize the piece. By Jorjanna Lundgren.
Collection, Diane Powers

Mandala jacket by Marilla Argüelles combines patchwork, appliqué, and quilting for a dimensional soft-work statement.

A pillow of mixed fabrics and tassels using appliqué with machine and hand stitching. By Diane Powers.

Simulated Seminole bands of pre-striped fabric are joined to create a unique skirt. By Frances Bardacke.

Embroidered detail of a hanging showing symbolic animals and figures. Guatemala.

Photo, Mel Meilach

Embroidery over a printed fabric, in progress, by a Guatemalan artisan.

Photo, Mel Meilach

Contemporary Seminole pattern. Detail of a skirt. By Marga Troha.

Beading and embroidery over a reverse appliqué mola for a blouse front (detail). By Diane Powers.

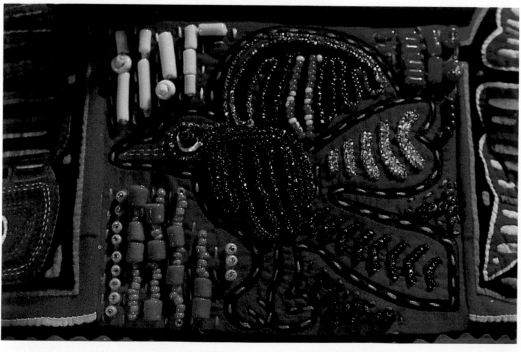

Barong dance costume, Bali, illustrates combinations of materials and the use of mirrors. Ideas and fabric usage may be developed from such ethnic costumes.

An intricately embroidered edging on hand-woven purple and white striped pants adorns the indigenous costume worn by the men of Santiago Atitlan, Guatemala.

Photo, Mel Meilach

Reverse appliqué soft-work mask is based on a Northwest Coast Indian wood panel. By Marilla Argüelles.

Rich embroidery, gold thread, and mirrors in a Balinesian dance costume can stimulate ideas for ethnic embroidery in combinations of prints, colors, and designs.

An abundance of ethnic needlework objects assembled from many countries are used throughout Diane Powers's home.

Cloisonné and silver beads of Morocco interpreted in stuffed and stitched satin fabric beads with metallic threads and pearl cottons. By B. J. Adams.

Photo, Clark Adams

A plain felt hat with a reverse appliqué panel from the Cuna Indians and woven strips with pompons from Guatemala. By Diane Powers.

Costume designers are always called upon to study clothing of other countries and periods, especially for productions that require foreign locales and historical settings. You can do the same. Analyze these costumes of Balinesé dancers and observe the cut of the garments, the combination of prints and solids, the linear designs, and the metallic elements in the headwear and trim. Think of using metallic threads in some of the garments you make along with fabric combinations that dare to be unexpected, yet compatible.

The *huipil*, a blouse worn by the women of Guatemala and Mexico, is essentially a rectangle that is doubled and sewn up the sides with an opening for the arms and the head. This young lady wears an embroidered huipil with a full skirt.

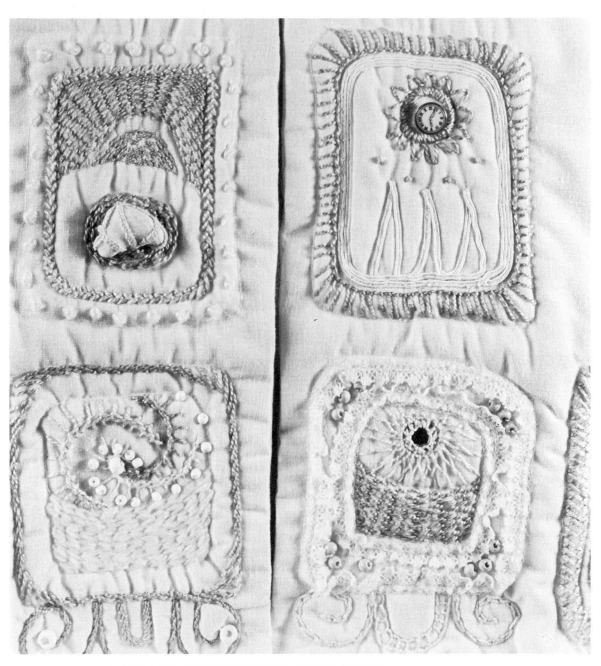

A circular cape with hood of white wool with white embroidery by Ellen Phillips *(opposite page)*, with details *(above)* from the front panel.

The circular shape represents the pre-Columbian Aztec calendar, and the embroideries around the hem and the front are interpretations of the carvings around the edge of the calendar. Similar motifs can be found in a stone stele and in architecture throughout Central America, such as the examples at left. Observe that beads and mirrors are used within the embroidery details though they do not appear in the original—an addition visualized and accomplished by the artist.

You can copy these designs directly, or use portions or repeats of them. Combine segments of one with those of another. Use mirrors, a medley of stitches, or a few simple stitches in a variety of colors, sizes, and textures.

From a Japanese border. Try Satin Stitches with shi sha mirrors or Spider-Web Stitch.

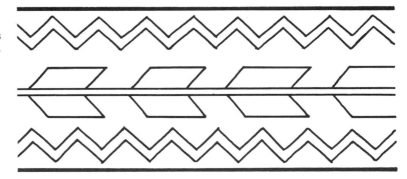

From a Japanese border. Try Straight, Slanted, and Padded Satin Stitching.

From a Russian embroidery. Perhaps Cross, Fishbone, and Roumanian Stitches.

From a Southwest American Indian border. Perfect for Running Stitches and machine embroidery.

Opposite page:
Dorothy Thelen made a magnificent wall hanging by embroidering over a printed fabric from an American Indian design. She appliquéd the embroidered panel to a solid backing of a complementary color. The brown, black, and beige material with wonderful geometric symbology has been enriched with a variety of stitches. Beads and a real arrowhead help carry out the theme. Approximately 36 inches high, 24 inches wide.

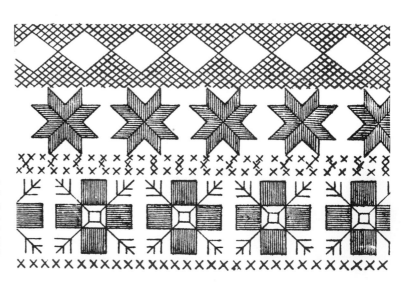

CUTWORK

You probably know cutwork by sight if not by name. You have seen it on doilies, handkerchiefs, lingerie, and tablecloths, as trim on delicate blouses and other wearing apparel. Cutwork, also called "Richelieu embroidery," was named for Cardinal Richelieu, who was eager to develop a needlework industry in France. He arranged for Venetian laceworkers to teach the technique, which remained in vogue throughout the seventeenth century.

Cutwork consists of designs that are surrounded by closely made Buttonhole Stitches and sometimes linked with bars; the fabric between the designed portions and/or the bars may be cut away. Today, cutwork may be combined with needle-weaving and any other fiber technique that will result in the appearance you want.

Detail of embroidered cutwork, by Rose Smith.

Photo, Dale D. Menagh

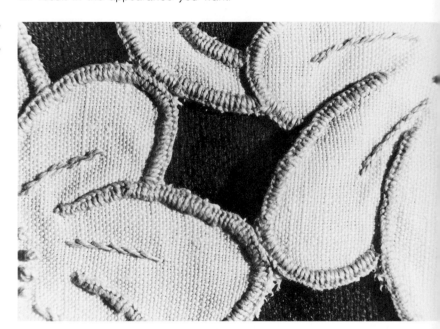

Draw your design on fabric. Outline the design with a Running Stitch, then cover the Running Stitch and the design edge with a Buttonhole Stitch worked very close together (it is shown wide apart on the drawing). When all design edges are sewn, cut away the backing, indicated by the shaded area, with a very sharp scissors, being careful not to cut into the stitching.

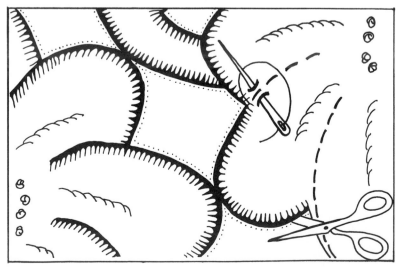

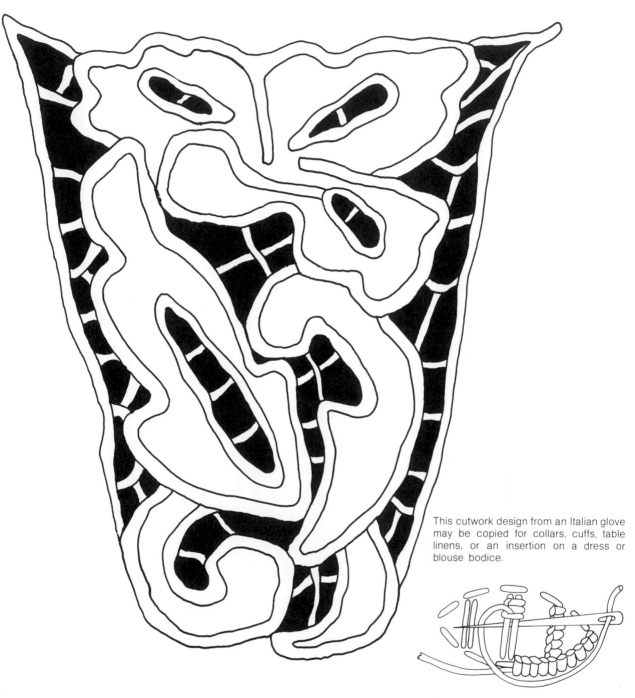

This cutwork design from an Italian glove may be copied for collars, cuffs, table linens, or an insertion on a dress or blouse bodice.

Many cutwork designs require the use of "bars." These are two or three lengths of thread used as "bridges" between the solid portions of the design to keep them from separating. Though they are utilitarian, they can be very decorative.

Make two or three stitches across the spaces and work Buttonhole Stitches onto the bars, as shown.

Traditional cutwork with bars used for the corner of a tablecloth. By Lillian Fisk.

Contemporary application of cutwork for detailing on a wall hanging with surface embroidery. Wools and cotton embroidery threads on a silk backing. By Dorothy Thelen.

Traditional floral cutwork. By Rose Smith.
Photo, Dale D. Menagh

Cutwork with needle weaving, embroidery, and beads mounted in an antique frame on weathered wood panels. By Dorothy Thelen.

Kid gloves from Italy are resplendent in the amount of cutwork used and the intricacies of the design.
Collection, Dona Meilach

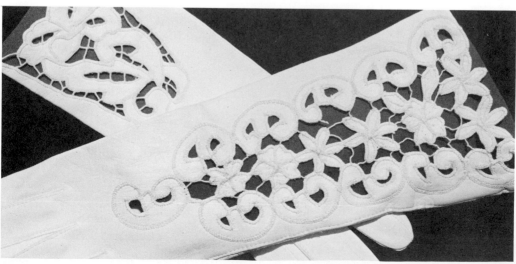

TAMBOUR WORK

Eighteenth-century needlework history books tell what tambour embroidery is all about. It is that old, and that new. Tambour embroidery is a continuous Chain Stitch worked through the fabric with a hooked needle; today we use a fine steel crochet hook. In olden days, tambour work was accomplished with special needles that you will probably find only as antiques.

Tambouring originated in the East and was introduced to France where it became a fashionable pastime for ladies in the eighteenth century. It was popularized when Madame de Pompadour had a portrait of herself, working with the tambour hook, painted about 1764 by François Drouais. In the painting, she worked at an oblong frame rather than the drumlike frame shaped like a tambourine from which the art gets its name.

Today, tambour embroidery is enjoying a revival. The reason? Many clothes imported from the Near and Far East display the detailing around the necklines and sleeves to create marvelous effects with a variety of yarns. Often the tambour stitch is used as a couching thread where it zigzags across heavier yarns to secure them in place. It could be equally effective on wall hangings and household items. It works beautifully for attaching beads and sequins.

An antique tambour frame resembled a drum and allowed both hands to be free. Today, the hoop is placed on a frame, or a quilter's hoop may be used.

Working Method

Tambouring must be worked in a stationary frame because both hands are necessary—one holds the hook, the other holds the thread. The thread is fed freely from a spool as opposed to working with cut lengths as in other embroidery. The ends of the thread must be secured; if they loosen, the entire embroidered length will pull out.

Hold the hook in one hand and the thread in the other. Both hands must work together. Insert the hook down through the fabric on the design line. Pick up a loop from beneath, as shown. For each stitch, insert the hook a short distance ahead, depending on the length you want the stitch to be, and draw through another loop, keeping the threads taut on the bottom. Secure the starting and ending points of the work, or the entire length of stitching can pull out.

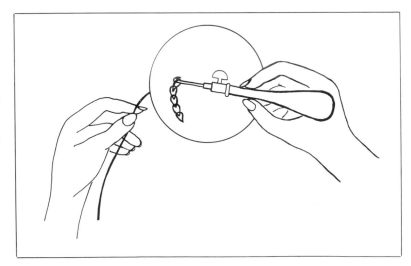

Dress detail of tambour stitching illustrates the intricate designs that may be accomplished.

A traditional Old Believer's dress embroidered with the Igolochkoy punch needle. The full blouse, called a "rukava," has embroidery across each shoulder; a jumper, the "sarafan," with embroidery on the bodice and skirt, is worn over the rukava.

Courtesy, Jean Cook

PUNCH NEEDLE EMBROIDERY

With the revival of interest in embroidery from various countries, what fun to uncover old techniques and tools! Jean Cook of California has probably been most responsible for bringing back Russian punch needle embroidery, a technique she learned from a group of Russian immigrant women. Called Old Believers (people who rejected Russian Orthodoxy during the seventeenth century and were excommunicated), they fled to various countries to escape persecution. They established isolated communities where they continued to intermarry and adhere to the social customs and dress determined by their beliefs.

Their traditional Russian dress is made from brightly colored fabrics and embroidered with Igolochkoy (ee-GO-luch-koy), a tiny closely looped pile embroidery accomplished with a special punch needle that looks and hooks like the rug punch needles used for larger work. The embroidery is also used for wall hangings, icon panels, and tablecloths.

Igolochkoy designs are almost exclusively colorful floral motifs, but contemporary embroiderers who have discovered the needle are broadening its usage to make miniature rugs, for placing abstract designs or lettering on fabric, and for combining the pile appearance with flat embroidery. The very finest punch needle is worked from the wrong side of any fine fabric with a single strand of embroidery floss, and larger punch needles are being marketed for use with threads other than embroidery floss, for a higher pile. Interestingly, the wrong side results in an attractive delicate flat embroidery design; the contemporary worker has discovered that either side is usable.

Punch needle embroidery may be accomplished with the Igolochkoy needle *(front)*, a tiny steel-handled punch needle used with fine threads. Larger punches may be used with heavier threads ranging from fine knitting worsted to thick rug yarn.

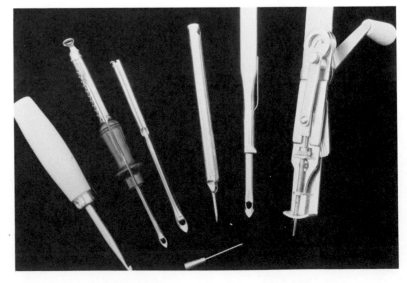

Punch work detail on a contemporary blouse from the Philippines based on a fifteenth-century royal garment (see p. 263). The panels are joined with crocheted Chain Stitching that pierces the fabric.

Collection, Dona Meilach

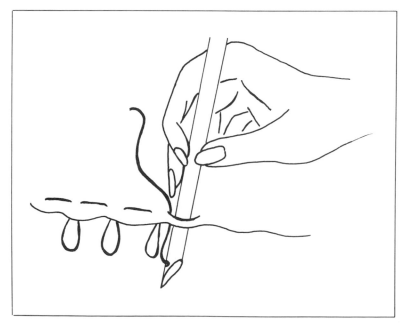

Punch needles using long strands of thread, or thread fed from a roll or ball, require that the fabric be held taut in a hoop or frame depending upon the size of the work (follow manufacturer's threading directions).

Rooster (detail) by Jean Cook illustrates looped pile that results from punch needle embroidery in the Igolochkoy tradition. This detail is blown up to about six times the size of the actual piece to give you some idea of the delicacy of the stitch.

Collar made with the Igolochkoy punch needle embroidery. By Selma Grossman.

A vest made by hooking yarns through fabric. The design was developed from decorations on a vase from western Europe. By Mimi Levinson.

This late-nineteenth-century American hooked rug detail of a lion could be a possible source for punch needle designs.
Courtesy, The Art Institute of Chicago
Bequest of Elizabeth R. Vaughan

Antique purse from Bokhara, Eastern Russia, was probably used to carry the Koran. It has a marvelous pattern that may be used with velvet, silk, or synthetic fabrics for a lustrous dressy accessory, or with rougher materials for a casual wardrobe.
Collection, Mr. & Mrs. Wayne Chapman, Solana Beach, California

Use the drawings of the flower motif and place them on the purse as you like. Add ribbon down the center and border edges and fringe at each side. The purse may be embellished with mirrors and buttons. A pile effect could be worked in certain sections with punch needles (page 68), or tambour embroidery might be worked around the edges with, or instead of, another treatment.

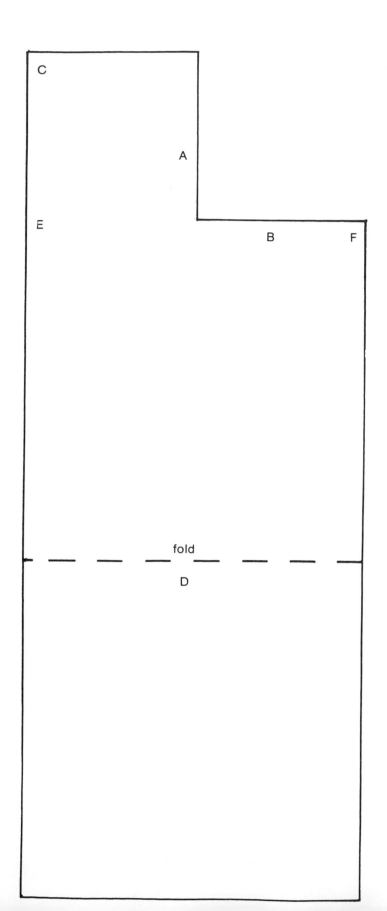

The Bokhara Purse pattern is made from a rectangle of fabric cut as shown. Adjust it to any size you prefer, allowing for seams as necessary. The extended top panel becomes the purse flap. A and B are sewn together so that C becomes the flap point at the purse center. Embellish as desired. Then fold the bottom at D so it meets the flap fold at the corners E and F. Fringe may be sewn between seams before closing, or added on afterward.

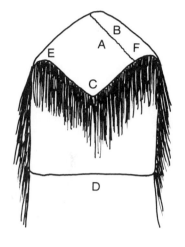

A machine-embroidered detail follows a carefully outlined pattern from Oaxaca, Mexico, worked by the Mixe Indians.
Photographed at
San Diego Museum of Man

Detail of free-motion embroidery from a skirt by Frances Bardacke. Usually the outline is stitched first, then the details are added. Although machine embroidery can be faster than hand stitching, it requires careful thought and planning before results are completely satisfactory to the discriminating needleworker.

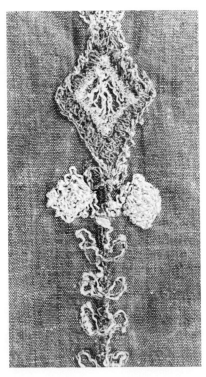

SEWING MACHINE EMBROIDERY

When ideas proliferate and there are not enough days in the week to accomplish all you have to do, you can turn to your sewing machine as your creative companion for exciting embroidery. Handwork is beautiful, lush, and time-consuming; machine work is beautiful, lush, and relatively speedy. The appearance of each is different, and each has the usual balance of advantage versus disadvantage.

Sewing-machine embroidery can be exquisitely detailed and versatile; the range of possibilities for stitch variations and patterns is incalculable. One stitch, for example, with different length settings, widths, needle sizes, thread tensions, and a few different colors can keep you busy experimenting and creating for days, probably weeks. Use different types of fabrics and it could be a lifelong study of potential. Add to this the many types of stitches possible with simple and more complex zigzag machines—a computer would blow its fuse figuring it all out.

For a beginning, learn the joy of creating with what you have. Machine stitching can be worked from predrawn patterns or it can evolve by "free motion," which means letting your needle and thread meander about the fabric, then looking at the design and filling it in any way you like.

Almost any kind of thread can be used for embroidery work, but the most predictable is 100 percent embroidery cotton. Use any fabric that a needle will penetrate, from fine netting and organza to thick upholstery fabrics and leathers.

When embroidery is accomplished with *the standard foot* in the sewing machine, the fabric should be placed on thin paper to prevent puckering; the paper is pulled away after the embroidery is completed. For *free motion* embroidery, *the foot is removed,* the fabric is placed in an embroidery hoop and manipulated in a design that can be loose and improvisational. Always learn what your machine and its attachments are able to do.

There are scores of books dealing with the possible range of machine embroidery (a few selected ones are listed in the bibliography). The examples that follow are offered to whet your appetite for machine embroidery if it is new to you. If you are already familiar with the possibilities, they will stimulate new directions, new ideas for patterning and designs inspired by various cultures. Some combine hand stitching with machine stitching.

In your own creations, try to incorporate ideas from more than one culture in one garment if the idea appeals to you. For example, a flower inspired by a crewel design from England can have a hand-embroidered mirror in the center with India as its cultural font.

A few of the infinite possibilities for stitch variations with the sewing machine. By Mandy Arrington.

A dress with machine embroidery by
Frances Bardacke has matching designs
on sleeves, skirt front, and hemline. The
colors are as bright and gay as the sun—
with linear designs and a geometry
inspired by a Mayan relief sculpture, (*far
right*).

Elements of the design, originally in stone, are simplified and drawn on paper, then transferred to the cutout fabric panels so they will be centered properly. Embroidery is finished before the pieces are sewn together.

Details of the dress *(left)* and the source of inspiration. By Frances Bardacke.

A ready-made plain cotton shirt from Mexico has been embellished with Chain Stitched machine embroidery on the shoulders, yoke, front, and cuffs and combined with hand embroidery around the shi sha mirrors and buttonholes. By Frances Bardacke.

Chain Stitching may be accomplished with a Cornelli or Singer chain stitch machine or with an old treadle type machine that does not require a bobbin. All details here are by Frances Bardacke and made with the Cornelli machine. The Chain Stitch is worked on cloth in a linear preplanned design. It can be squiggled in a free motion technique and combined with other embroidery stitches.

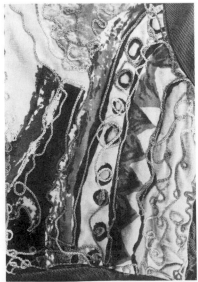

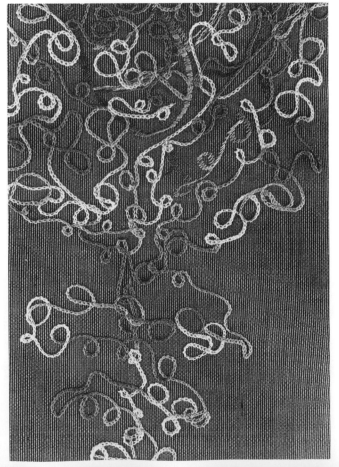

Nan Ferrin used a variety of cams on her machine to produce the stitches on the hand-blocked panel appliquéd to a shirt back *(detail, below left)*. The circles were block printed with a carved potato dipped into fabric dye; then the various types of embroidery were developed.

Machine embroidery is effective when it is placed on sleeves and the back in unusual patterning for a man's jump suit. Designed by Michael Lane.

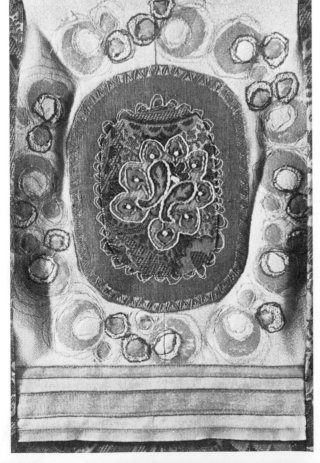

A machine-stitched pillow created by Diane Powers in cotton corduroy is fun to make from the pattern given and a perky addition to any collection of interesting throw pillows. The zigzag Satin Stitch, made with a zigzag machine, is used for filling between and at the edges of the appliquéd details. If you do not have a zigzag machine, you can improvise with hand stitching. Refer to the photo of this piece (illustrated in the color section) for possible color combinations.

The face (detail). Straight machine embroidery is used for the nose, eyelids, and mouth outlines, machine appliqué for the cheeks and hair. Hand-embroidered Satin Stitches are used in the eye details.

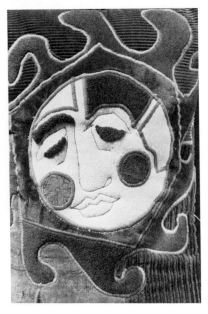

A purse called a "pick" pocket is made to hang around the neck as an ornament and also to hold a guitar pick. The pattern is placed over the fabric, then filled in with machine zigzag Satin Stitches. By Sheila Smith-Swaidon. The design was suggested by the Hopi Indian basket (above).
Basket photographed at San Diego Museum of Man

Leopard head by Karen Spurgin worked in hand and machine embroidery with appliqué and beads. It was inspired by a painted plaster animal head made by African artisans.

MORE PUT-TOGETHERS

Combine ideas and fabrics from many sources to add your own touch of eclecticism.

Embroidered fabric from a Mideastern tablecloth found at a house sale was refashioned into an overblouse designed by Barbara Chapman.

Collection, Dona Meilach

A sachet holder *(below)* from China with Satin Stitching could easily have been the conscious or subconscious inspiration for Tina Connally's heart-shaped embroidered pendant *(right)*.

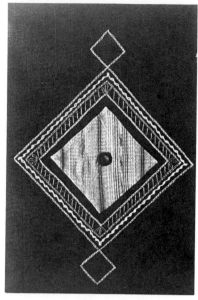

Elisabeth Schimitschek's overblouse pulls its inspiration and materials from many sources: hand-woven fabric from South America is appliquéd with embroidery added. The sleeve detail *(above)* repeats the image of a god's eye, usually made in wrapped yarns. The same type of detail *(below)* appears in the embroidery of the Syrian dress shown in its entirety on page 44 to illustrate how similar designs exist in different cultures.

Carol Emerick isolated one detail from a Czechoslovakian floral design and embroidered it onto the pocket of a cotton denim shirt.

Right:
A lushly embroidered child's bolero from Poland.
Photographed at the Milwaukee Public Museum, Milwaukee, Wisconsin, by Dee Menagh

The surface embroidery on a coiled raffia purse from Mexico offers another style of flower.

Printed flowers from English crewel designs are loosely interpreted for the stitchery on a purse made from a pair of blue jeans, and for a stand-up soft decoration. By Foy Beck.

Tina Connally interprets the swirls and fully filled-in design of a silk sash from Southeast Asia *(above)* in an overall layer-upon-layer embroidered soft cushion *(left)*, using a variety of stitches.
Sash, Collection,
Mr. & Mrs. Wayne Chapman,
Solana Beach, California

Linda Jones adapted a pre-Hispanic design for the embroidery on the front of a casual shirt *(left)*. The pillow *(above)*, made by Nancy Pichler from woven upholstery fabric, has an embroidered ancient Mexican motif.

4. Appliqué Adds Up

ADD ONE LAYER OF FABRIC ON TOP OF ANOTHER IN A VARIETY OF shapes and materials and what is the sum? High-fashion appliqué, when the common function is an ethnic derivation. Appliqué, from the Latin word "applicare" and the French "appliquer," means "to put on," "attach." It has appeared in too many cultures to count, and possibly as early as 3000 B.C. in ancient Egypt and Asia. Among some peoples it was men's work, in others, women's work. In some countries, such as Bolivia, both men and women traditionally worked at the art of creating their costumes with appliqué.

Examples of objects using fabrics added onto one another are as obvious as the heraldic symbols, tents, flags, and banners used by the early Romans. In Tibet appliqué was essential for creating awnings, saddle blankets, wall hangings, and clothing.

The materials and threads used for appliqué are as unlimited as its potential. Early Canadian Indians and Eskimos used moose hide as appliqué and the moose hair for the embroidery thread and detailing. North, Central, and midwestern American tribes are known for their "ribbon" appliqué, which is considered a "modern art" dating from the late 1700s. Brightly colored ribbons were appliquéd in stripes to a dark foundation. In the finest work, geometric shapes were cut from the ribbons, then both the cutouts and the remaining strips were hand-stitched in a new relationship to a contrasting background. The technique has inspired hundreds of projects in current needlework magazines, using the wide variety of plain and embroidered ribbons available today.

A brief geographic survey of appliqué over the past two hundred years in various countries yields wonderful imagery applicable to contemporary work. Animal and human figures on wall hangings from Dahomey, Africa, illustrate a simplicity and gesture not unlike the marvelous shapes a child might draw. From Hungary, you will find bold designs on clothing in felt, leather, and heavy wool that are easily suitable to detailing for the Western world. Leatherwork from Africa and Greece can also be adapted in both design and material.

Elisabeth Schimitschek appliquéd colored fabrics to create a wall hanging based on motifs and gay colors of the Hawaiian Islands. Shapes are appliquéd to an embossed ground fabric, and embroidery is added with a variety of stitches.

87

In far-flung corners of the earth, women quietly work at their sewing machines to create appliqués for their own clothing, for tourists, and for export. A Thai woman assembles geometric patterns of small diamond shapes around a Cross Stitch panel.

Appliqué from other countries can be developed in spectacular dimensions in addition to the design ideas. Actual pieces of old and new embroidered fabric, sewn by the people of those countries, can be cut apart and added to modern garb. The Greek dress designer Yannis Travassaros, in 1973, introduced a stunning dress with a front yoke panel and matching handbag made from fragments of "sperveri," elaborately embroidered bed curtains from the Cyclades and Dodecanese, and immediately sent other dress designers scurrying among townspeople everywhere for fabrics that they could buy and apply in similar fashion.

Using the same concept, you may discover wall hangings, bedspreads, clothing, and accessories from other cultures that are already composed of appliquéd materials. Visualize portions of these pieces dismantled, recut, and used in a new way on something you create. Often the material itself will spark an idea.

Appliqué is a mode of needlework whether or not it is combined with embroidery. It requires sewing by hand or machine. The method may vary: in some traditions the edges of the applied fabrics are carefully turned under and blind stitched, in others the edges are turned under and the stitches are allowed to show as part of the design. In the 1960s one saw appliquéd parts with raw edges protruding, and often purposely frayed, for textural and visual interest. Depending on your design, all appliquéd

An appliquéd repeat design on a table runner from Thailand can be cut apart and re-appliquéd for borders on solid color skirts and blouses. Portions could be stitched onto a jacket or used for the front and back of a tabard with tie ribbons or strips of woven fabric from another country. One piece of material may spark your imagination for many possible combinations.

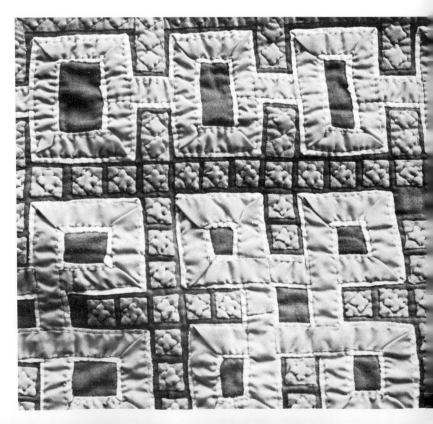

materials can be secured by yarns or by a variety of decorative threads shiny and dull, thick and thin, straight and zigzag. They may be further embellished with beads, buttons, and shells.

Adding various patterns and shapes of materials to one another is a good warm-up method for patchwork, quilting, and dimensional soft work shown in later chapters. As you delve further into needlework sources, you may discover:

"*Broderie perse,*" or "*Persian embroidery,*" also called "cretonne appliqué." It consists of printed fabric motifs cut out and stitched to a ground fabric with minimal needlework and a result similar to the pieces by Diane Garick Mergenov on pages 108 and 109.

"*Broderie suisse,*" also called "shadow appliqué," is accomplished by inserting a piece of fabric between a semi-transparent top material and more solid background material. A stitched design is made through all three pieces of material, but the inserted motif (usually in a shape different from the top and bottom fabrics) shows through as a shadow or a hint of color. We show you how to do it on pages 110 and 111.

"*Padded appliqué*" results in a relief dimension. The applied fabric is lifted from the background and lightly stuffed. See Chapter 10, page 196.

"*Reverse appliqué*" involves the combination of several layers of fabric and the designs are cut back through one or more layers to reveal layers below. See Chapter 5.

Stitches used to add one fabric to another can be functional and decorative. Make them bold to match or contrast with the cloth, or hidden, if you prefer. A detail from a floor cushion by Elisabeth Schimitschek has fabrics that are smooth and rough, tight and loosely woven, and appliquéd with large contrasting color stitches.

The individual designs on a nineteenth-century American quilt can be emulated in today's fabrics and appliquéd for clothing, wall panels, bedspreads, or updated versions of antique quilts *(detail). Courtesy, The Art Institute of Chicago*

APPLIQUÉ METHODS

You can design fabric shapes on a piece of paper, then transfer them to cloth, or design directly on cloth. The size of the fabric piece will differ if you use a raw edge or a turned-under hem. For hem turn-unders the following procedures are basic.

1. Cut the shape with an additional ⅛- to ½-inch allowance all around for hemming. Fabrics that fray easily, such as velvet, may require a larger turn-under. Experiment. Mark the seam allowance with a dressmaker's tracing paper and a tracing wheel or with a row of machine stitching on the back of the shape.

2. Clip into the seam allowance on all edges and at corners. For interior and exterior curved edges make tiny slits at angles as shown. Turn in the seam allowance and the marked edge of machine stitching, so that it will not show when it is reversed. Press the seam down on the wrong side.

3. The shape may be blind-stitched using a fine thread and taking stitches close to the edge of the appliqué.

4. Or an obvious Running Stitch can be used to hold the shape in place. Large decorative Chain Stitching, Long and Short Stitches, Feather, and any variety of stitches may also be used.

5. The piece may also be machine-attached with a zigzag stitch.

Large appliqués are often easier to work on a large piece of stretched fabric rather than in small embroidery hoops. Cover an old picture frame that has *thin* molding; thick or wide molding prevents working close to the edges. For hangings, the outside fabric edge can be the frame, or the mounted fabric edge can be covered with a decorative molding.

1

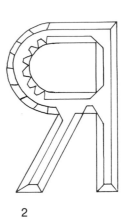

2

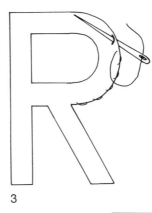

3

4

5

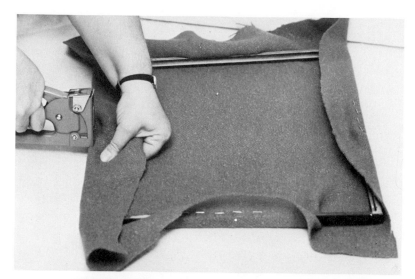

Place the frame on the fabric in the direction of the weave, not diagonally to it. Staple the *center only* of the fabric on one side, then pull from the center on the opposite side and staple. Do the same with the third and fourth sides so the fabric is stretched drum tight.

Trim the fabric at the corners, leaving about a 2-inch edge. Pull the center fold taut; make two or three tiny folds rather than one large one, and staple.

"Four Mile Polychromed Bowl," from Homolovi No. 1 near Winslow, Arizona, offers excellent, clear-cut, linear shapes adaptable to appliqué and embroidery. The zigzag painted design could be interpreted with rickrack, braid, or ribbon.
Courtesy, Field Museum of Natural History, Chicago

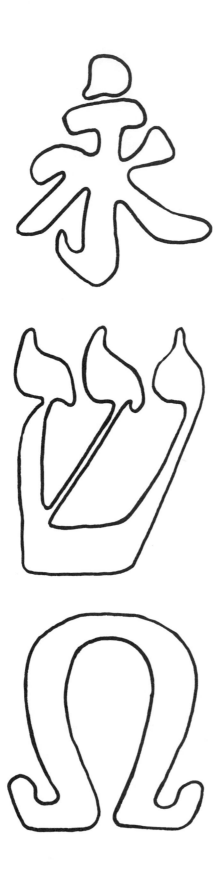

Opposite page:
An enlarged detail of Elisabeth Schimitschek's Aloha Banner (page 86) illustrates various methods of appliqué and embroidery. The appliquéd flower petals are turned under and blind-stitched. Backstitching forms a decorative outline. French Knots are clustered in the center. Leaves are outlined with Feather Stitching. The letters, made of felt, do not have turned-under hems, and they are appliquéd with a variety of decorative stitches.

Different alphabets are marvelously adaptable to exotic embroidery. Try Japanese, Hebrew, and Greek letters in various styles; use portions or stylized designs based on them. Books on calligraphy offer myriad suggestions for the use of alphabets in design for clothing and wall hangings.

The same shapes and their details may be appliqué onto ethnic garments such as a "Szŭr," the festive coat worn by Hungarian cattlemen. The coat, cut much like a kimono, can be created in heavy materials for an outer garment, or in light materials for an opera coat, lounging robe, or hostess gown.

A Portuguese sidewalk mosaic (above) can be a mind-boggling clothing inspiration. Joan Hamilton appliqued felt shapes to a blouse neckline and used an embroidered line of Back Stitching to contain the design.

The design above and the entire hanging (opposite page), or portions of it, can be used to create appliqués. To duplicate these or other designs in the book for which a pattern is not given, use the following procedure:

1. Trace the design from the book with tissue paper (or photocopy the page).
2. Use carbon paper to transfer the design to graph paper.
3. Alter the design to the size you need for the project, using the methods for enlarging and reducing on page 13.
4. To carry the design (above) around the front of a garment, repeat the pattern or alter it as necessary to fit the parts.

An alternate method is to photocopy or draw the design, then have it blown up by the blueprint process to the size needed. Trace the design directly on fabric with a dressmaker's tracing pencil. Look in your Yellow Pages under Blueprinting for this service.

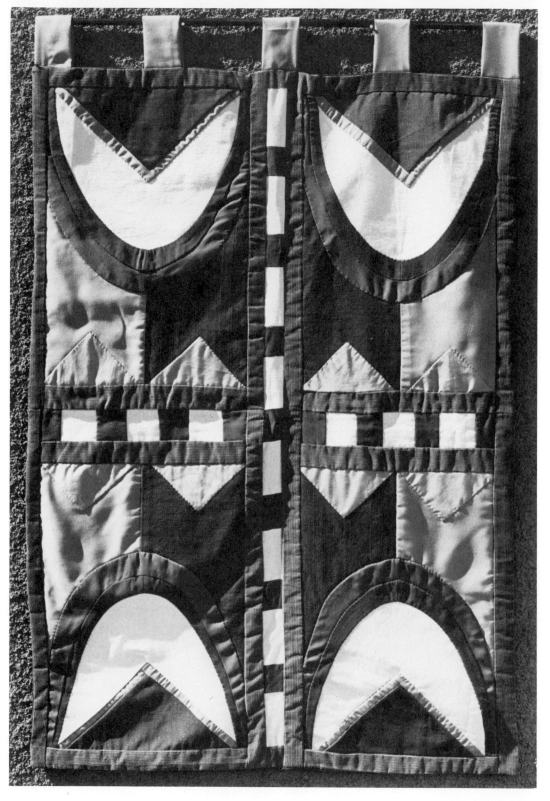

A wall hanging adapted from a Dakota Indian parfleche (rawhide) case. Marilla Argüelles appliquéd gold, olive, and wine-colored cottons on a muslin background. 36 inches high, 26 inches wide.

Kachina dolls, made of carved wood and painted, are created by the Hopi Indians of Arizona for the religious education of their children. Claire Jones studied the head of the doll *(below)* and captured the graphic design in fabric that she appliquéd onto the back of a blouse.

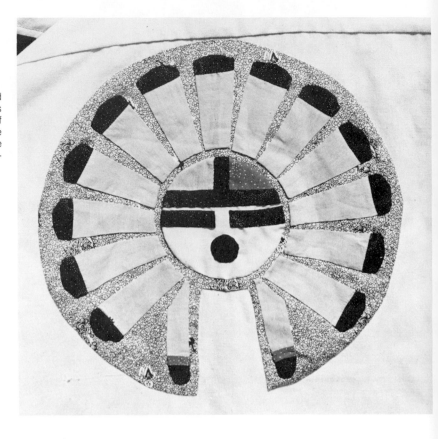

Tawa (sun) Kachina doll of the Hopi Indians of Polacca, Arizona. The design on the sash as well as the face could readily be used for embroidery or appliqué.

Photographed at
San Diego Museum of Man

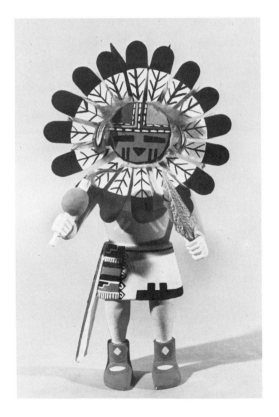

Beverley Stefanski's wall banner also simulates a Hopi Indian sun symbol seen on a coiled tray *(below)*. Beverley's symbol is machine-appliquéd cotton with Satin Stitching on one panel of the banner, which is reversible. It may be hung in a doorway and viewed from both sides. Braiding and tassels are added for a festive look.

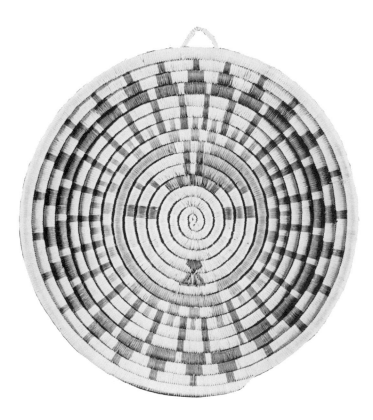

Hopi tray.

Photographed at
San Diego Museum of Man

Nancy Pichler consulted a book of ancient motifs of Mexico and the result was a bird appliquéd onto the back of a vest with an original touch the Mexicans, and probably no one else, would ever have thought of. The bird's body, wings, and feet are made from two pairs of kid gloves. Can you recognize the "fingers" as the birds' wings and tail feathers? The head is suede with facial features made from parts of the glove. The vest front has a crochet panel with stitchery, and a matching neckband with a suede collar.

Drawing of an ancient bird motif used for vest design above.

Use the Mexican bird design for your own interpretations in fabric, or any of the marvelously simplified shapes used in the pottery designs of Indian cultures.

From San Ildefonso

From Zuñi

From Acoma

From Hopi

*Drawings from
Decorative Art of the
Southwestern Indians
by Dorothy Smith Sides.
New York, Dover Publications, Inc., 1936.*

A contemporary appliqué panel from Colombia, South America, is typical of that country's folk art. Simple figures are appliquéd with little concern for perspective. Embroidery fills in much of the background. Your children's drawings could be copied in fabric and appliquéd for a personalized wall hanging for their rooms, or for charming individualized details on their clothes.

Collection: Mr. & Mrs. Wayne Chapman,
Solana Beach, California

METAMORPHOSIS #1. A wall hanging by Wende Cragg is adapted from an ancient Oriental design which had cut paper work in the center. It is machine-appliquéd of velveteen and corduroy.

Courtesy, artist

Appliqué with embroidery using a Mexican Indian design. By Linda Jones (detail below).

Appliqué is integrated into the design of a batik fabric by the Meo peoples. Panels are assembled and used for the back, yoke, and front of a sleeveless coat with straps used for carrying a baby.

A black, pink, red and white hat worn by children of the Meo Hill tribe, northern Thailand *(above)*, was dismantled and the parts stitched to a contemporary blouse *(left)*. It is wise to wash the appliqué before attaching permanently to be sure colors are fast and will not ruin the garment. When in doubt, dry-clean. By Dona Meilach.

A black dress from Thailand has strips of colorful fabric overlaid and appliquéd to the front, sleeves, and side slits. Edges are finished with rickrack and a decorative running stitch.

Collection, Dona Meilach

Nancy Inman adapted an aboriginal jacket worn by the men of west central India, and added a personal symbolism based on native ideas she learned while living in the East. Called MY LIFE JACKET, it uses all old fabrics. Pockets fascinate her; some have zippers, some have perforations "to allow one's spirit to get in and out." The lining *(below)*, cut from a man's shirt, is hand-embroidered with adages and symbols, and has more pockets. Measuring tape, used as a ribbon trim, represents a "measured side of life." Velvet indicates intuitive aspects of life. Fabrics include Thai silks, drapery swatches, cottons, cotton corduroy, and a neckband woven in Thailand.

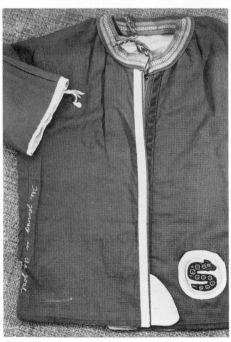

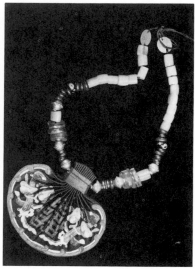

Carol Martin's sleeveless jacket is an Oriental coat pattern which she embellished with ribbon appliqué and hand embroidery.

An antique Chinese sachet is trimmed with ribbon and pieced fabrics, combined with antique beads, and made into a handsome pendant. By Diane Powers.

An adaptation of a North African man's coat with hood is made of lightweight fabrics with hand-print material and ribbon appliqué. By Carol Martin.

RIBBON APPLIQUÉ

A visit to a museum concerned with American Indian lore can reveal techniques you may have overlooked until your eyes zero in on the needlework of different cultures. In the late 1700s several Indian tribes, using the same observations and inspiration from other cultures that we employ today, developed a "ribbon work" for which they became very well known and respected. It was believed to have evolved from the clothing of Spanish missionaries; it appeared on the skirts, robes, moccasins, leggings, doll clothes, and carrying bags throughout the Plains and Woodland regions. Different groups used distinct design motifs and characteristics; often beading was added to the ribbon work.

The simplest designs were made of strips of silk ribbons or crisscrosses that simulated commercial printed and woven plaids. More involved designs usually imitated the traditional beadwork in geometric and floral designs attributed to the specific tribes.

The finest work was accomplished in a unique way and is most "collectible" and valuable today. Geometric shapes were carefully cut out of the ribbons. The ribbons were hand-stitched to a dark background so the ground would show through the cutout areas. The cutout pieces were then hand-stitched on the ground adjacent to the ribbon from which it was cut. The result was a complex-looking, yet simply executed, positive-negative design. When several layers of the cutouts were combined, the appearance was like a broad appliquéd border for elaborate skirts, and along shawl and robe edges.

Many variations of Indian ribbon work can be developed today because of the huge range of exciting ready-made ribbons on the market.

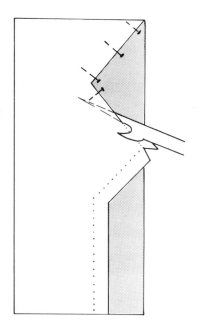

To turn under ribbon edges evenly and easily, run the tip of a seam ripper along the edge and pin the turn-under in preparation for blind stitching.

Above and right:
Indian ribbonwork is usually geometric; cutouts may be planned by carefully ruling on paper, then transferring to the ribbon. The cut-away ribbon pieces may be re-appliquéd or folded before cutting completely to appear as mirror-image positive-negative designs on each side of a panel.

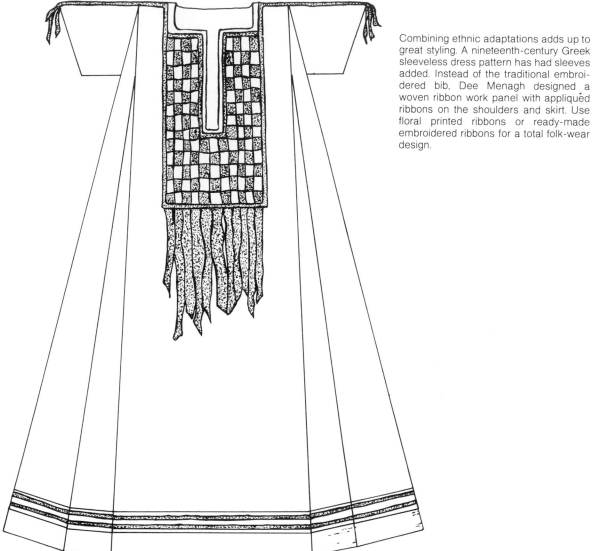

Combining ethnic adaptations adds up to great styling. A nineteenth-century Greek sleeveless dress pattern has had sleeves added. Instead of the traditional embroidered bib, Dee Menagh designed a woven ribbon work panel with appliquéd ribbons on the shoulders and skirt. Use floral printed ribbons or ready-made embroidered ribbons for a total folk-wear design.

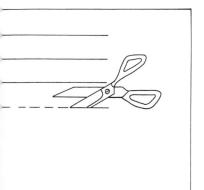

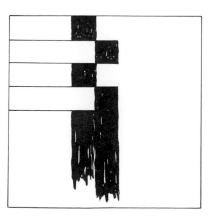

Cut horizontal slits carefully in the dress bodice as far apart as your ribbon is wide. Weave the ribbons through the slits from top to bottom allowing the ends to hang loose at different lengths. Carry a ribbon border trim around the neckline and at the top shoulder, allow ends to hang, and attach beads or tassels if desired.

FABRIC MOSAIC

Diane Garick Mergenov creates a unique statement in hand-sewn clothing that is a blend of elaborate Byzantine mosaic design and American appliqué. Each of her "fabric mosaics," as she refers to them, is developed over a foundation skirt or jacket. She selects about six fabrics that will work well together, usually recycled from other clothing, and cuts two or three large shapes. She then pieces and designs smaller parts that will overlap each other. The design builds up as she works. All edges are carefully finished and the insides of the garments are as much a work of art as the outsides. The garment (*opposite page, top right*) is completely made of dress labels perfectly matched in a symmetrical design that resembles the patterning of a Byzantine stained glass window. (See additional examples in the color section.)

Interiors of jacket edges, skirt waistbands, and skirt slits are finished with exquisite care and detailing (*above and opposite page, far right*).

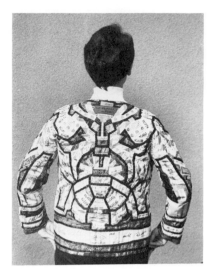

SHADOW APPLIQUÉ

Textile curators and authors often differ as to definitions for techniques that have been handed down by generations of needleworkers and historians. "Shadow appliqué" seems to fall into this "shadow" of definition category. To make identification and definition easy in terms of contemporary embroidery, think of shadow appliqué as a "sandwiching" technique using three layers of material. A middle layer of a shaped, brightly colored material is sandwiched between a bottom layer of opaque fabric and a top layer of sheer fabric. Stitching is accomplished through all three layers to result in a muted center layer that shows through the sheer top.

It is not complicated, but it is very effective. The sheer top layer allows shimmers of silk, glistening satins, or brightly colored under-fabrics to catch light and create exciting shadowy effects.

Use your own updated version of shadow appliqué with flat fabrics, or you can pad lightly beneath the middle layer (like putting mayonnaise on bread) to give an extra lift to the form and create a deeper shadow on the surrounding materials. Shadow appliqué can provide exquisite detailing on clothing and wall hangings. It is a creative challenge with such readily available sheers as nylon hosiery, netting, loosely woven muslin, and other open-weave materials.

Delicate table linens, made with only two layers of fabric, a sheer and an opaque, are also often referred to as "shadow" appliqué.

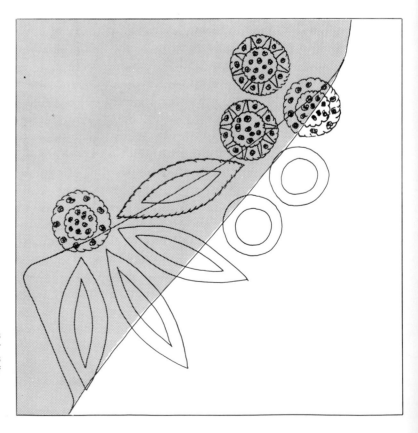

Shadow appliqué consists of shapes placed on a base fabric and a sheer fabric placed over them. Embroidery is worked on top of and through all layers of the materials.

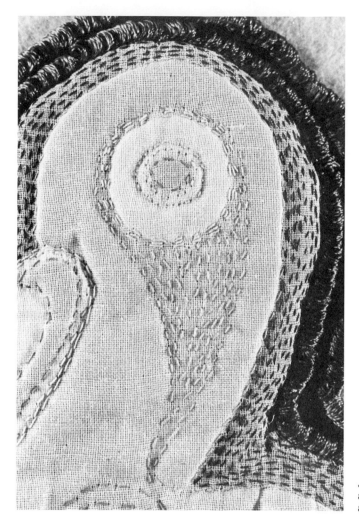

Jill Spurgin embroidered a whimsical animal using organza on top of felt appliqués (detail).

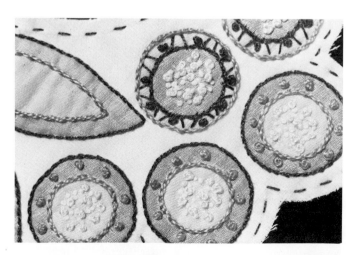

A detail of a collar made with hot pink felt shapes were laid on white cotton and covered with white organza. French Knots, Back Stitches, and Straight Stitches were used for the complete collar. By Dee Menagh.

Hand-painted parasols are an indigenous craft form in many of the Far Eastern cultures. A Thai worker's art is an American needleworker's inspiration *(right)*.

Hazy, mysterious forms under brightly colored umbrellas are created with shadow appliqué. Figures are only suggested beneath the netting. By Elisabeth Schimitschek.

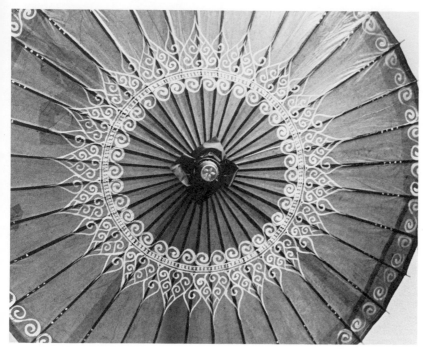

The patterns on Oriental hand-painted paper parasols are adaptable to shadow appliqué. Try a solid-color fabric background, then a layer of shiny pink, dark blue, or purple with a top of sheer veiling material. The stitching can simulate the parasol's ribs and hand painting. Develop any size from small appliqués on clothing to large wall hangings.

Drawings from Central European peasant embroideries can be utilized for attractive shadow appliqué.

LACY AND LOVELY

Lace doilies, portions of curtains and tablecloths, fringes from shawls, and embroidered white work are as kindred to the ethnic look as apple pie and ice cream are to America. With old doilies, antique and new portions of net, crochet, and knotted work (anything goes) appliquéd tastefully to clothing and costumes, you can be downright naughty, or delicately nice. The lacy look may be used with other appliqué materials: with beads, mirrors, and surface embellishment sewn on by hand, and machine-embroidered stitches. Lace, sheer, and white-work pieces are also adaptable to shadow appliqué shown on the previous page.

A wedding hat by Jorjanna Lundgren uses a lacy doily as shadow appliqué with a hand-embroidered edge, and a lace trim for a subtle veil. Embroidered lettering on the satin ribbons are wedding homilies.

The corner cut from a lace-fringed shawl is appliquéd to the front of a ready-made shirt from India. Stripes of floral print fabric are embroidered along the front and sleeve. Closely matched floral hand-painted beads are added to the fringe and made into a matching necklace. By Dona Meilach.

Detail of a bodice front with a lace panel and hand embroidery. By Twyla Cottrell.

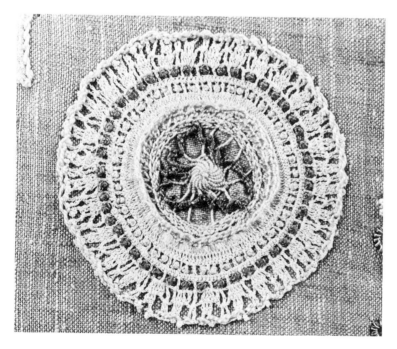

A portion from a lace tablecloth has been cut out and appliquéd to a skirt with hand embroidery. By Frances Bardacke.

Commercial machine-made lace with Bullion Knot roses is appliquéd onto the front of a tunic blouse (detail, *right*), and used for the sleeves. Lace edging trims the bottom. By Elisabeth Schimitschek.

Carefully composed, appliquéd antique lace doilies are combined with shi sha mirrors and embroidery for a delicate overblouse (detail, *right*). By Elisabeth Schimitschek.

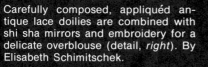

Tatted and crocheted antique lace is appliquéd onto a plain tunic, front and back, in an attractive and different arrangement. Floral print fabric on the sleeve is repeated in the neckline facing. By Vini Sozzani.

A costume designed by Leon Bakst for the ballet "Le Dieu Bleu," in the early 1920s, has a lacy-lovely look with ovals, circles, and other geometric shapes. Every panel offers abundant ideas for appliqué and embroidery.

5. Multi-ply, Subtract, Add = Reverse Appliqué

ADDING LAYERS OF FABRIC TO ONE ANOTHER IS APPLIQUÉ, AS described in Chapter 4. Subtracting layers is referred to as "reverse appliqué." The process usually involves placing multiple layers of fabric on top of one another, then purposely cutting back to reveal the layers beneath in various shapes and progressions.

The technique can be more flexible than tradition offers. After layers have been built up and cut back into, you can again add portions to any section of the appliqué. To carry it further, you can add the entire panel to skirts, blouses, handbags, and hats, and for infinite decorative purposes. You can use the panels themselves to create garments by fashioning them into something else and, perhaps, adding other needlework portions to them. Once your mind begins to calculate the potential of this arithmetical approach to appliqué, your answers can never be wrong. You can create a new formula that is uniquely your own function.

The reverse appliqué panel has become almost synonymous with the mola, a blouse created by the Cuna Indians of the San Blas Islands, which are about a mile off the mainland of Panama. The panels attached to the blouse, front and back, are often elaborate and brilliantly colored. One mola panel may be made of two to six layers or more, of different colored fabric. The layers are cut back to reveal one or several beneath, with the edges of each layer carefully turned under and hand-hemmed. All the space is filled in and embroidery may be added.

To the Cunas, the mola is the major form of needlework, and also their means of displaying wealth. A San Blas maiden would have at least a dozen or more new molas in her dowry.

It is intriguing to study the transformation the Cunas' indigenous motifs have undergone as a result of contact with the outside world. Missionaries, personnel from the United Nations, military, and tourists introduced magazines, calendars, and comic books to the islands. The women, who certainly cannot read all the languages, adopted the often-repeated printed images as a magical symbology. Words and logos copied loosely from foreign advertisements appear in the appliqués. A penguin from a cigarette ad of the 1960s is an abstract bird motif laid over the letter "w." There are airplanes, a helicopter with claws, and canned food labels. The "Orange Crush" mola panel on the following page combines reverse appliqué with added portions over some of the letters for better design definition.

Reverse appliqué is not solely the domain of the Cunas. The Meo Hill tribe of northern Thailand exhibit the technique that they have handed down for generations, but the designs are always repeated and symmetrical, not nearly as bold, naive, and imaginative as those of the Cunas. There is evidence that the craft was also practiced by early Egyptians and some African tribes.

Reverse appliqué panels made by Liz Zimch are a modern adaptation of the mola idea from the Cuna Indians. Liz made her own designs from four layers of colored felt, then appliquéd them to an overblouse for a unique, stylish touch.

119

Observe the marvelous abstraction evolved by a Cuna needlewoman for the reverse appliqué panel based on an "Orange Crush" advertisement. All spaces are filled in; the design is asymmetrical. Letters are used as design rather than message (detail *below*).

Photographed at
San Diego Museum of Man

A shadow puppet used in the Balinese theatre can be adapted to a reverse appliqué design using two or more layers of fabric.

THE MOLA METHOD

The San Blas reverse appliqué panels are usually made of plain color fabrics stacked one on top of another and basted together in a loose grid starting from the center out to keep the fabrics flat. The experienced needleworker does not draw her designs, but rather clips the top layer with a fine embroidery scissors, carefully cutting away the shapes and folding back the edges to reveal the color beneath. Later, she may use these cut-away sections to poke under other areas and stitch into place to appear as additional layers. The turned-under edges are usually pinned and then sewn with a tiny hemstitch using a matching color thread.

To emulate the mola technique, follow the general instructions. Experiment with two or three layers of fabric until you are familiar with the method and can achieve neat, carefully sewn designs. Then you are free to depart from the rules and make up your own formula. You might like edges that are not turned under—where the unraveling becomes an additional texture. The use of small pieces of print fabric can also be eye-catching, especially when it is tied in with a repeat of the design in other accessories. Appliquéd rickrack and shiny ribbons can be incorporated for detailing.

For fabric, use felt for a simple way to create the design, as you will not have to tuck back and hem the edges. Poplin or sailcloth is excellent; pure silks and shantung lend themselves beautifully to the technique. Corduroys and rough woven fabrics are good for large designs, as the tuck-unders need to be wider. Suede, leather, and synthetics such as vinyl and ultrasuede can also be used effectively.

Three layers of fabric are cut back so that they show under one another in the reverse appliqué technique. The right side *(top)* is the design; the back side *(bottom)* illustrates the stitching and the layers. By Louise Hinds.

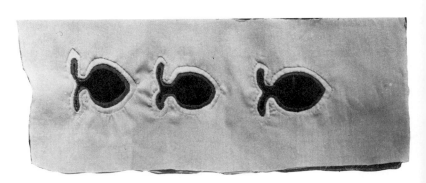

Baste three layers of fabric together.

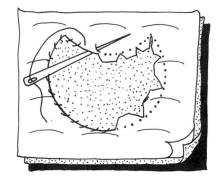

Outline your design on the top layer. Cut it out and hem it under to reveal second color.

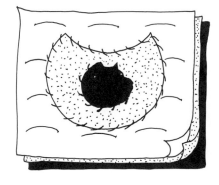

Indicate a smaller cutout area within the second color. Note that the circle to be cut at this point is smaller than it will finally appear because you must allow for a turn-under.

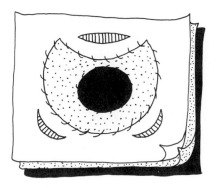

Cut the circular shape from the second color to reveal the third color and hem. You may add appliqué shapes on top of the first color (or elsewhere) to make it appear that there are additional layers.

Linda Jones' handmade purse is a perfect show-off idea for your own reverse applique panels. Felt cutouts are easy to work with because you achieve instant results without a great deal of hemming. Add shapes on top of some layers, too, as Linda did for the whimsical bugs (see below). An oval of felt forms the bugs' bodies; heads, legs, and details on the backs are embroidery.

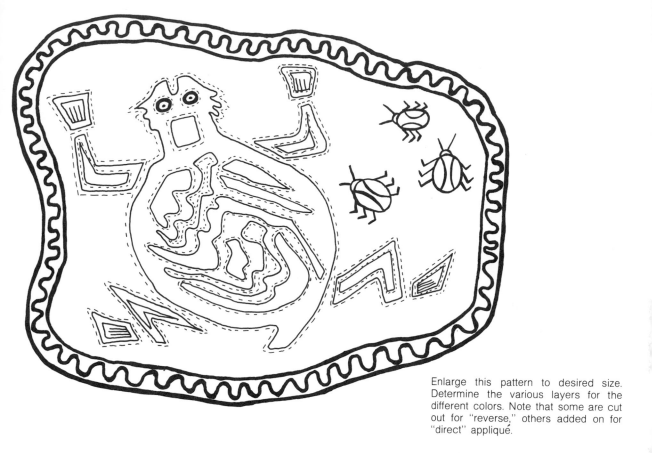

Enlarge this pattern to desired size. Determine the various layers for the different colors. Note that some are cut out for "reverse," others added on for "direct" appliqué.

Use Chilkat blanket designs from the Northwest Coast Indians as inspiration for ethnic designs in felt.

Simplify designs and make them in felt for use on a wide variety of objects. The following will give you a start, and possibly inspire novel and practical uses for attractive needlework accomplishments.

A tree of life created by a Cuna needleworker. Layers are often composed of scraps of old materials recycled. Use the tree of life pattern below for a beginning and add as many layers as you like.

Photographed at San Diego Museum of Man

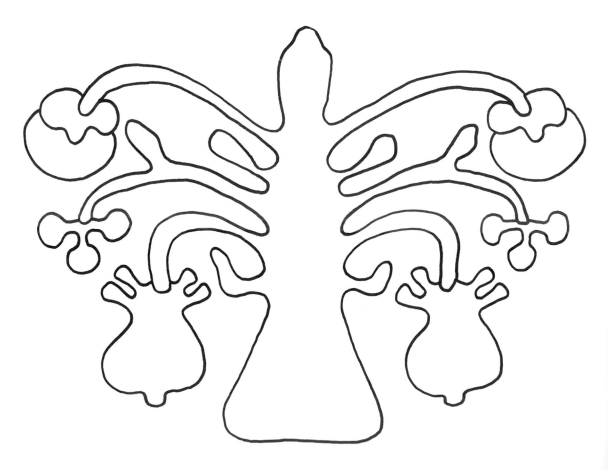

Almost any design can be used, whether it be a sophisticated work of art or a funky little bee. Jackie Van Dyne appliquéd a panel made of felt onto the back of a woolen shirt.

Elisabeth Schimitschek used one tiny detail from a Cuna mola and enlarged it in felt for an attractive book cover.

Mandy Arrington integrated a square panel onto the front of a pillow, outlined it in braid, and added tassels at the corners.

Virginia Black exposed five layers used for the abstract floral design; you can see them each neatly hemmed at the edges. They form a repetition of color that is additionally carried out in the embroidery within and around the outer pillow edge.

A round panel can be developed in reverse appliqué with a design concentrated in the center. Areas are left free of design, unlike the Cuna molas where every inch is filled in. By Elisabeth Schimitschek.

Opposite page:
Detail of the pillow (*right*) illustrates the effective use of embroidery in a contemporary adaptation of the native technique. By Elisabeth Schimitschek.

Old mola panels found in secondhand shops are often dull and worn looking. Elisabeth Schimitschek worked an outline of bright Chain Stitching around shapes and immediately transformed the panel into a fresh piece which she appliquéd to the front of a blouse.

Use portions of old panels or begin anew with your own selection of fabrics to make reverse appliqué. Pre-Hispanic Mexican stamp designs are perfect: these can incorporate rickrack if you like.

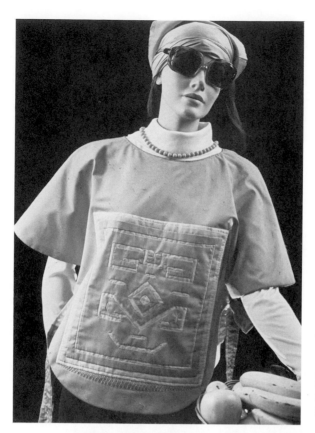

Elisabeth Schimitschek's cape-sleeved tabard is cotton shantung, an easy material to use for a two-layered appliqué in orange and pink (detail of design below). An effective row of Herringbone Stitching integrates the straight edge of the panel with the curved edge of the garment.

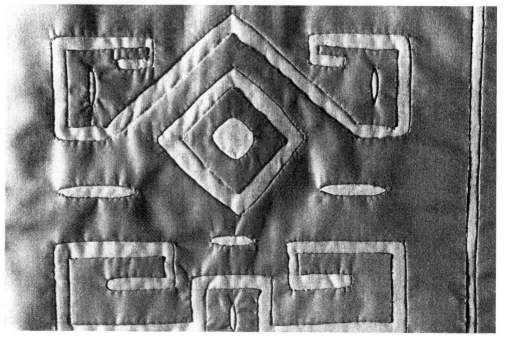

Details *(below)* of the dress *(opposite):*
It is hard to out-think Elisabeth Schimitschek's innovative approach to reverse
appliqué in a modern mode. Anything
goes, but with a creative restraint so that
all the parts become a fashionable,
original entity. The white cotton dress is
crisp and colorful with pink, orange, red,
solid and print fabrics, rows of lace, and
hand embroidery.

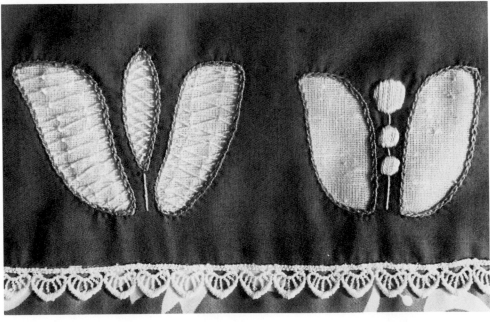

Margie Robison made a skirt and short tabard top to match. The skirt has a mola panel on the bottom; similar coloring appears on the hand-embroidered mirrored panel used on the tabard. Additional panels with complementary hand-printed designs are appliquéd, and the result is as artistic as a Mondrian painting.

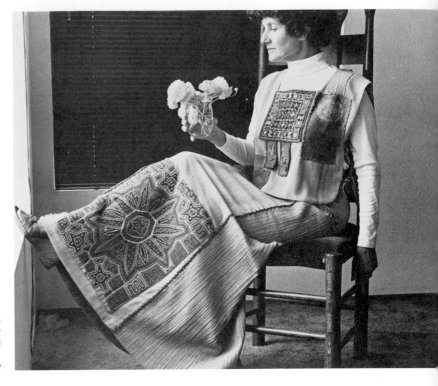

Below, right:
A kettle-cloth tunic by Joanne Purpus employs tucks on the sides, a few mirrors, and part of a mola at the top and sleeves.

Courtesy, artist

Below:
A colorful mola is appliquéd to the front of a handmade skirt by Eileen Bernard. Rectangles, made with bright embroidered and printed ribbons, integrate the panel so it does not appear as an afterthought.

Two vests by Diane Powers employ the entire mola panels as though they were pieces of fabric. Ready-made braiding is used around the sleeves and neckband for trim; the linings are beautifully developed with fabrics that relate in color and design to the exterior print.

A casual purse with a round wood handle has a small mola with personal symbolism within. By Frances Mehic.

A dressier purse handmade by Mary Hardy incorporates a ready-made mola with bands of ribbon appliqué, embroidery, and beading. Handles for purses are available where craft and needlework supplies are sold.

Jorjanna Lundgren uses molas to create softly padded boxes to hold jewelry, sewing supplies, or personal treasures. Portions of materials from other countries all add up to a colorful decorator item with an original touch; the fabrics may include pieces of Guatemalan woven bands and an East Indian table runner. An attractive ceramic pendant or bead is used for a handle.

Collection, Diane Powers

Sharon Griswald evolved an inspired use for a felt reverse appliqué to enrich a living room corner. She created a semicircular panel, mounted it on a piece of wood cut to the same shape and placed so the straight edge of the panel is butted against the wall corner. On the adjacent corner a mirror the same size as the panel reflects the mola and gives the illusion of a full circular panel.

Opposite page:
Eleanor C. Smoler created a series of panels placed in a box and lit from behind. She calls them "Lycons" and thereby gave birth to another original adaptation of a mola. Colorful cotton is layered and the cut-throughs are made from front and back to achieve a desired variety of tone and translucency. They are placed against a multi-faceted plastic panel used as the box front; a fluorescent light tube is mounted within the box. The result is a brilliant stained-glass effect in a unique medium.

Courtesy, artist

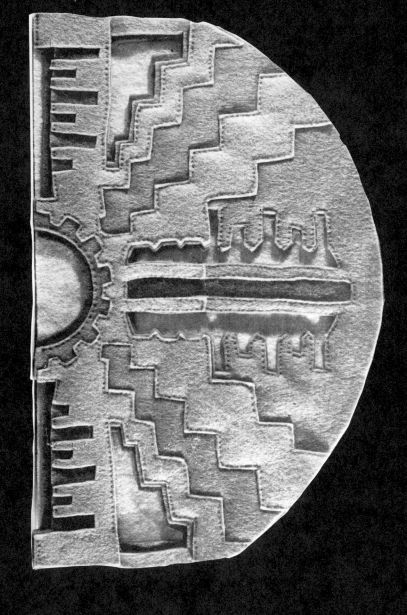

The tympanum of a Spanish church has stone-carved designs ideally suited for interpretation in reverse appliqué.

6. Patchwork Potential

MENTION "PATCHWORK" AND MOST PEOPLE WILL CONJURE A picture of a multipatterned quilt and clothing dating from the late 1880s in America. And rightfully so. It was then that the practice of recycling scraps of worn clothing and leftover materials from current sewing projects evolved as a typically American craft. As nostalgia from the past has become increasingly popular, needlework magazines have offered marvelous ideas and instructions for re-creating traditional patchwork for quilts, dresses, handbags, household accessories, and other useful items.

Rather than tread over well-worked ground, we are presenting less publicized, more obscure patchwork styles, including the novel patterns inspired by the Seminole Indians of Florida.

You will also find traditional patchwork ideas that have been exploded and combined in myriad inventive ways. And, for readers interested in history, even patchwork is not wholly unique to early American ecologists. In her book, *A World of Embroidery,* Mary Gostelow states: "It is thought that patchwork originated in the East about 3,000 years ago, and one of the earliest examples is a leather canopy, c. 980 B.C., in a collection in Cairo. In Sir Aurel Stein's archeological surveys at the Caves of a Thousand Buddhas in Serindia, North India, he discovered fragments of patchwork curtains and hangings believed to be from the same period."

A tunic shirt with a peasant blouse neckline and wide sleeves becomes a stunning garment when it is trimmed with carefully cut printed triangles repeated in the same progression on a complementary print background, then edged with ribbon appliqué. By Frances Mehic.

The past history of patchwork can offer inspiration for more flexibility with materials, styling, and patterning. The concept of borrowing ideas from many peoples and combining them to develop new approaches to needlework offers a powerful springboard for the potential of patchwork.

141

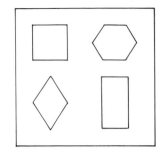

1. Templates and the resulting patches have geometric shapes so the edges can be butted up to one another: squares, hexagons, diamonds, and rectangles.

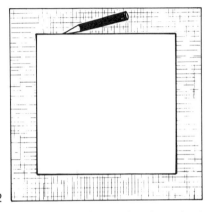

2. The template is placed so the grain of the fabric is at right angles and a tracing line is made on the fabric. Two patches may be cut simultaneously, but more than that may result in slightly uneven-sized pieces.

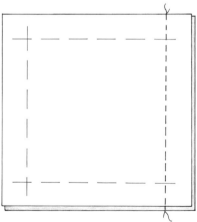

3. The seam allowance is marked. With the grains of the fabric running in the same direction, sew the first two patches together by machine or hand with a running stitch. Press the seams open.

4. Add patches to make lengths. It is best to work from the center out.

5. And then expand. In this manner the patchwork shapes evolve into a large piece of patchwork fabric. When working with different colors and patterns, lay out the design and number the squares on the back in the order in which they are to be arranged.

BASIC PATCHWORK PROCEDURES

Patchwork is almost always created with regularly cut geometric fabric shapes because they can be pieced together easily. They should be precisely cut with the warp and weft of the fabric at right angles to each other. A template, made of cardboard or heavy clear plastic, should be used. Templates are available commercially or you can cut your own. A clear plastic template allows you to move it around and select a design in the fabric that you may want to use in a specific way. You should have two templates of the same shape—one the size of the patch, the other smaller for marking the ¼-inch seam allowance.

Variety in color and visual excitement can be increased tremendously by cutting the individual shapes in halves diagonally or in smaller geometric progressions and then rearranging these parts with portions of the shapes cut from contrasting fabrics—always allowing for seam joinings.

The patchwork seams may be assembled by machine or hand. Additional hand embroidery is often worked over the seams or into the patterns. Patchwork used for quilts, coverlets, or wall hangings may be interlined or padded as with quilt making. Select proper fabrics for the specific project. Closely woven materials that do not fray are recommended for functional clothing and household items. Use cotton percale, broadcloth, and muslin; avoid rayons, nylons, or flimsy fabrics.

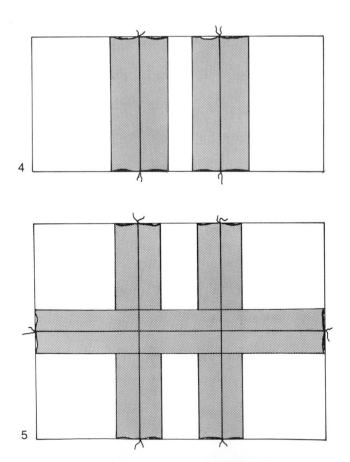

BIRTHDAY DRESS 1976. Bucky King. Composed of 776 fabric pieces in prints and solids of red, white, and blue. Observe the variety of patchwork shapes within one garment; some purposely hang beyond the fabric for a novel treatment.

Courtesy, artist

A simple square shape can be tremendously varied as illustrated by this dress from Thailand. Thin strips of appliquéd fabric edge the patchwork panels.

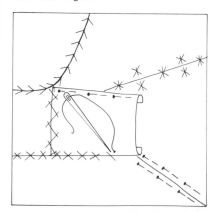

A "crazy quilt" is so called when patches are made of uneven shapes. Patches may be joined with a variety of stitches, as in this detail from an early American coverlet.

Collection, Roger Brown, Chicago

For "crazy quilt" patches, shapes are pinned together and decoratively hand-seamed to camouflage and unify the necessarily uneven joinings, which may have raw edges.

LOG CABIN PATCHWORK

Log Cabin patchwork is a very old American design that is as ideal for contemporary needleworkers as it was for our ancestors. The use of fabric strips laid in a clockwise direction yields an optical illusion of deep space depending upon the arrangement of tones and colors. Through the years, there have been many variations in the colors used, but the procedure remains the same. It begins from the central square and evolves outward. It may be used for quilts, wall hangings, pillow covers, purses, pocket details, and wherever else your creativity can make it work. Try a single very large log cabin square for an entire wall-treatment "headboard," with matching bedspread in smaller log cabin squares.

CUTTING AND ASSEMBLING A LOG CABIN SQUARE

Use Diagram 1 for your cutting and assembling pattern. The center is a 2-inch square. Each strip is 1 inch wide and varies in length according to pattern. The overall block indicated is 8 inches. Larger blocks can be made by adding more strips to the outside of the diagram or by making the center larger and each strip wider.

To begin: Cut cardboard templates for each strip, as shown. You will need to make templates for the following strips only: 1, 2, 3, 5, 7, 9, 11, 13. When making the templates, always add a ¼-inch seam allowance to all edges. Cut or tear fabrics to equal the lengths and widths of the templates in your planned color sequence.

To assemble: Strips can be sewn to each other, or they can be assembled onto a foundation fabric. Follow the sequence as shown, beginning with the center square and working outward. Place the pieces with the right sides together and join them, working clockwise until the entire block is pieced.

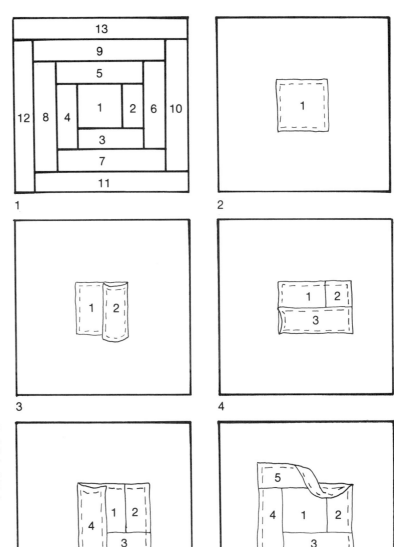

Log cabin patchwork purse by Jill Spurgin in tones of faded and dark blue denim with eight strips on each side.

An Early American example of patchwork (detail), using a square within a square.
Collection, Roger Brown, Chicago

Pieces of silk ties were cut into strips and made into squares. The squares were assembled in the patchwork mode for an overall coverlet.

Collection, Lillian Bryce

SEMINOLE PATCHWORK

A solid-colored skirt is bordered with modern interpretations of Seminole patchwork. Narrow and wide geometric bands are alternated with solid bands and rickrack. By Berrylynn Freeby.

Seminole patchwork is soaring in popularity. The intricate geometric patterns have a flickering vibrancy; they are attractive and a delight to create. Yet they are very simple. There are bands of solid color alternated with strips of design bands. The design bands are strips of colorful fabric sewn together, then cut and resewn in a new relationship.

We show you the so-called "secrets," and with one or two principles of pattern understood after your first Seminole patchwork project, you will be able to arrange the colorful bands in any way you like. Use them for belts, purses, skirts, pillows, bedspreads, chair covers, details, trims, or entire jackets. Use shimmering fabrics for dressy occasions, sturdy washable cottons and synthetics for those items that will take a great deal of wash and wear. Ribbons and bias tape can be used for narrow patterns.

We suggest that you glue colored strips of paper onto a backing paper; cut them into segments and rearrange them in the patterns shown here, or any of your own. Once you see the relationships of the parts to the whole you'll be able to make myriad designs quickly and easily. You can also simulate some of the design bands by using striped fabric, then cutting it apart into new arrangements. But the traditional Seminole designs are made by sewing together the strips of color and rearranging them.

THE PRINCIPLE IS SIMPLE

a. Sew together three horizontal strips of fabric all the same width, then cut on the dotted lines vertically.

b. By laying each strip on a slight angle the pattern of the total strips changes.

a

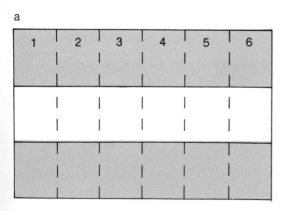

b

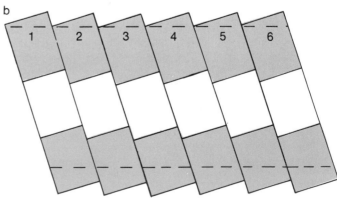

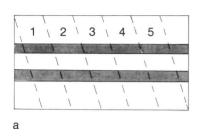

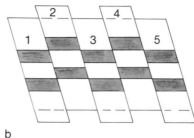

a. Five strips of fabric, of different widths, are sewn together horizontally, then cut at a 65-degree angle.

b. The odd-numbered strips stay in position; the even-numbered strips are lifted so the darks and lights alternate and a new pattern results.

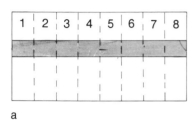

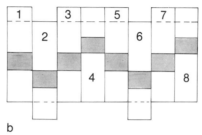

a. One narrow strip is horizontally sandwiched between two wider strips and then cut vertically.

b. In rearranging, the odd-numbered strips remain in position. Numbers 2 and 6 are dropped. Numbers 4 and 8 are turned upside down for a different arrangement of the rectangles.

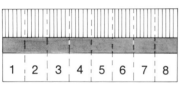

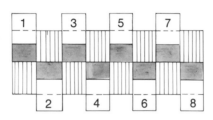

a. Adding one striped fabric in the horizontal bands results in another possible change of appearance. Three strips are sewn horizontally and cut vertically.

b. The strips are rearranged so that the even-numbered strips remain in position. The odd-numbered strips are turned upside down and raised.

A series of solid and striped bands are cut and tilted and remain in the same relationship; but they are interspaced with a verticle solid band with embroidery. Raw edges are decorated with a zigzag machine stitch.

Opposite page:
Kathy Whitaker wanted to emulate a Seminole jacket, so she made her pattern from one in the museum where she worked, then created patchwork designs as closely as was practical, shown in the details top and bottom. The geometric band at the top is composed of three horizontal strips, cut vertically and tilted to form triangles. The band, below, is made of four horizontal strips cut vertically and interspersed with a light-colored narrow vertical strip and a dark-colored wide vertical strip.

A patchwork jacket made by the Seminole Indians of Florida, probably fairly recently, has a full blouse back, wide shoulders, and a pieced underarm. The patchwork elements are interspaced with solid bands of satin appliquéd with rickrack.
Collection, Roger Brown, Chicago

Detail of the center band from the above jacket.

An intricate, beautiful skirt in Seminole patchwork on black velvet. Though so many geometric shapes are used, the result is not confusing because of the unity provided by the velvet background and the repeat rickrack. By Marga Troha.

Patterned fabric makes an interesting departure for Seminole patchwork. Instead of rickrack, the artist used hand crochet for the narrow white horizontal motifs. (detail, *left*). The skirt *(below)* by Gladys Moore.

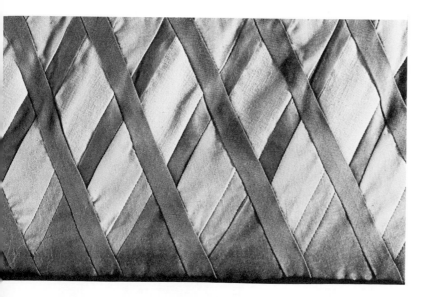

Detail of a pattern using eight horizontal strips cut on an angle, tilted, then each strip alternated with a solid strip to create the diamond-shape pattern. Each narrow strip is bias tape; the wider strips are colored fabrics. By Muriel Towle.

As if to prove the earlier statement that designs appear around the world in different cultures in variations, the purse *(below)* from Thailand has triangles and strips in patchwork progressions not unlike those of the American Seminole Indians. The purse pattern itself is so simple to assemble and so practical that we offer it to you here. Make it in any fabric you like and embellish it with the patchwork patterns shown, with Seminole patchwork, or with embroidery. Use a complementary color fringe, or a border developed with wrappings and tassels shown in Chapter 12.

cut two

10"

8"

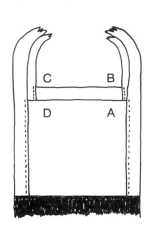

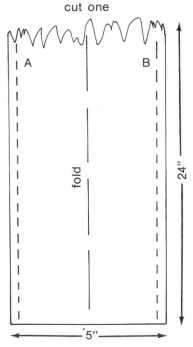

cut one

A B

fold

24"

5"

C B

D A

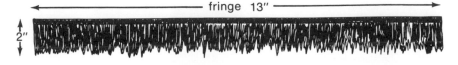

fringe 13"

2"

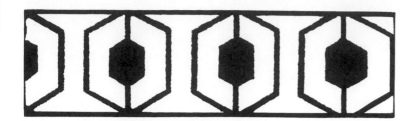

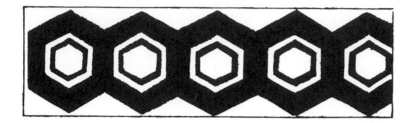

Designs from Japanese borders offer stimulating ideas for patchwork shapes, shapes within shapes, and geometrical relationships for Seminole patchwork.

7. Silver and Gold; Beautiful and Bold

AH, THE LURE OF PRECIOUS METALS. THE LUXURY, THE SHINE AND shimmer that silver and gold threads impart to the embroidered surface make them hard to resist. And there is no reason that you should resist them if the lustrous tones are those you want for your creations.

Metal thread embroidery wends its way through history and stirs exciting imagery: royalty dressed in velvet and silk robes heavily encrusted with swirls of gold; church vestments displayed in glass cases and brought out on special occasions; the opulence of the costumes of Cleopatra and her maidens.

Metal threads are actually made of gold and silver, although today many synthetic fibers are available. A variety of threads would include:

JAPANESE GOLD: Finely beaten and cut gold coiled over a core of very fine silk floss thread. It has a warm, rich color and does not tarnish. It does tend to unravel and must be handled carefully. There are several varieties, diameters, and qualities of gold and silver thread. Buy whatever you can for an inventory to use when the need arises.

PURL THREAD (called bullion) is coiled and looks like a fine metal spring. When purl thread is couched onto a fabric it has the appearance of a Bullion Knot. Purl is available in different thicknesses and types. ROUGH PURL has a dull satin sheen. SMOOTH PURL has a shiny finish. CHECK PURL has a checkered appearance because it is bent into angles before it is coiled. PEARL PURL is coarse and stiff; it is usually associated with military and club badges.

SYNTHETIC METAL THREAD will not tarnish, but the surface has an even, cold shine compared with the warmth of real metals. The two can be combined effectively.

BRAIDS, STRINGS, and CORDS, in gold and silver color, are easy to find, not nearly so costly as the real thing, and have many applications in decorative work.

Metal threads are almost always couched to a surface, and the fabric should be stretched taut over a frame or it will pucker and the threads will not lie flat and smooth. Fine threads, such as synthetic Lurex, can be used as sewing threads and with a sewing machine. Some metal thread can be used with needlework canvas; the enlarged mesh is easier to pass through than tightly woven cloth. Usually pulling metallic threads through fabric causes them to unravel or break.

The delicacy of fine metal threads requires special handling, and some may tarnish or change color from the oils in the skin. Use white gloves or a tweezer and work over a piece of dark felt or velvet so cutoff pieces will not jump away. Store the threads, wrapped around a soft tube of felt, in airtight containers to prevent discoloration. Keep the work between acid-free tissue paper used by jewelers, and store finished garments carefully for the same reasons.

Pairs of gold threads couched onto a wool backing outline an appliquéd figure on the detail of a wall hanging from Burma, mid-1800s. Twisted threads are used in some of the interior areas. Observe that the facial features are created with couched metal thread also. The complete hanging (shown on page 3) illustrates the combined use of metal thread with appliqué and embroidery.
Collection, Julanna Loveberg, El Cajon, California

155

MATERIALS:

Metal threads for embroidery are available in skeins, on spools, and on cores. They include elasticized gold and silver twisted cord, flat braid, and various purl threads. The needlepoint-covered box is accented with metal thread. Elasticized thread worked in a detached Buttonhole Stitch holds a polished stone (see page 160). By Ruth Colt.

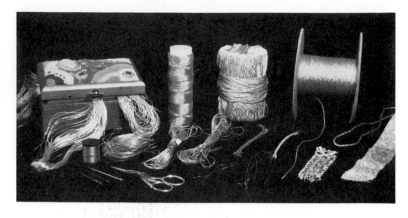

METHODS FOR COUCHING METAL THREAD INCLUDE:

1. Flat metal braid is often adhered to the backing with a blind stitch. Curves require careful manipulation of the braid.

2. Simple couching. The metal threads are placed on the backing material and a needle with a couching thread is passed over as many strands as desired. The stitches may be close together or widely separated in rows one above the other or in a brick pattern as shown in the sampler.

3. Ends of the metal threads should be pulled through to the wrong side of the fabric to hide them. Put the end of the metal thread through a needle with a large enough eye and pull the thread through the fabric to the underside. If necessary, poke a hole through the fabric with a dressmaker's stiletto or awl.

Flat braid and round metal threads are couched in different patterns of stitching with sewing thread.

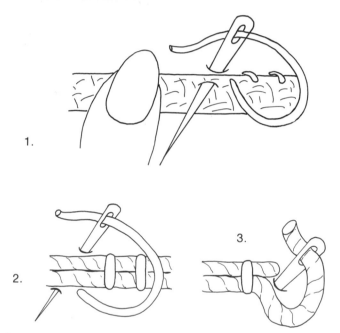

1.

2.

3.

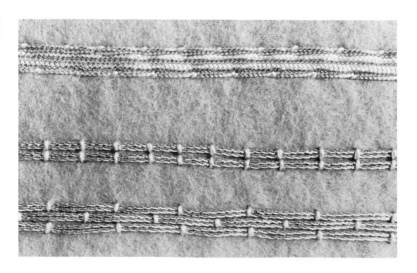

A Chinese pleated sachet with couched flat gold braid developed in a calligraphy design.

Private collection

Flat gold braids and twisted cords define the linear elements in a Burmese panel from the mid-1800s. Silver sequins stitched to the fabric simulate the peacock's feathers; the peacock body is padded and raised.

Collection, Julanna Loveberg,
El Cajon, California

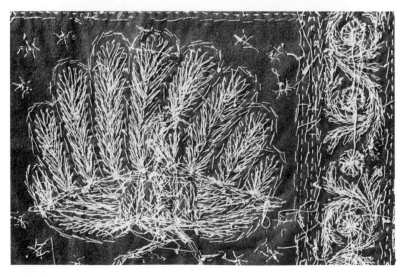

The back of the panel *(above)* illustrates the thousands of tiny stitches used.

The examples that follow will suggest many progressions for metal threads and the couching stitches so that they can be both decorative and functional.

The design on a bronze Chinese pot from the early Chou period can be imitated as a motif for couched metal threads. The design can be used for clothing borders or for any decorative accessory.

Script lettering used in medieval times is defined and couched with gold thread on a green velvet purse. Gold thread is also used for the macramé trim and handle. By Elisabeth Schimitschek.

Gold thread on black velvet (detail, *right*) is used as the central design of an epaulet from Manchuria. The threads repeat the etched design of the metal banding (*above*).

Photographed at
San Diego Museum of Man

Detail of doll (see color plate). An embroidered panel of antique gold thread was cut up and portions of the fabric assembled onto the doll for a royal garb. By Diane Powers.

A small detail from the flower of a Chinese silk robe with intricately embroidered borders (*above, top*) was the idea source for the framed wall hanging (*above*) by Mandy Arrington. Mandy delicately hand-painted the fabric (detail, *left*) with cold-water fabric dye. The flower was padded in the trapunto method, and silver thread was couched as an additional combination of cultures and techniques.

A belt detail from Afghanistan serves as an example and design source for individualized uses of metal threads in your own garments. Use the pattern below to embellish a purse panel or a neckline, or enlarge it sufficiently for a pillow, book cover, or other accessory.
Collection, Mimi Levinson

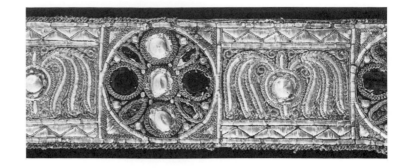

A gemstone may be secured to the surface of a fabric with a detached Buttonhole Stitch to simulate a metal cabochon. The stitch is worked with elasticized metal thread from around the base of the stone upward and far enough to hold the stone as in a piece of metal jewelry. Additional decorative embroidery may be worked around the base. By Ruth Colt.

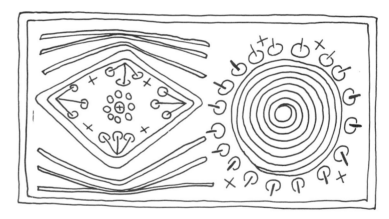

Gold purl (bullion), a springlike metal thread, is couched onto a satin collar in a diamond and circular shape with other detailing added. The pattern will help you arrange a similar motif on fabrics and objects of your choice.
Collection, Dee Menagh

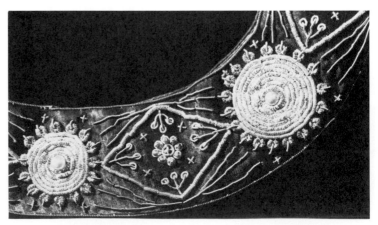

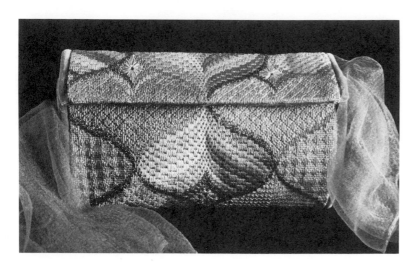

NEEDLEPOINT WITH METAL THREAD

In needlepoint the threads are sewn through the mesh backing rather than couched on as in embroidery. Therefore, choose threads that will not break readily; work with short strands in large-hole mesh. In all these examples, the gold thread is an accent for the wool needlepoint yarns. By Ruth Colt.

8. Bead-azzling

BEADS HAVE BEEN A PART OF OUR CONTEMPORARY CULTURE in so many ways that we tend to take them for granted. They actually came to us in a roundabout fashion. White traders brought beads to America where they were used as money, known as "wampum," and exchanged for furs and skins with the Indians. The tiny glass or china pieces made in far-off Italy by the Venetians were quickly integrated into Indian crafts. They replaced the berries, shells, teeth, and claws that had been used extensively. For beadwork designs, the native women turned to their traditional craft of quillwork and emulated the same or similar patterns with beads.

Beadwork among the Indians developed in different stages. The oldest and earliest efforts were necklaces made of simple single-strung strands. Probably in about the early to the middle 1800s, beads began to be used as an embroidery element; the strings of beads were sewn onto backings using an Overlaid, or Couching, Stitch. The stitches themselves were probably learned from embroidery techniques brought by the colonists. The type of bead, the availability of threads, and the stitches used varied from tribe to tribe. Embroidered beadwork appeared on clothing, moccasins, gloves, belts, travel bags, leggings, and other objects.

Woven beadwork, the process of weaving lengths of strung beads onto warp (illustrated on page 167), is more recent. Early Indian weavers improvised a bow with a number of warp strings placed in the position of the bowstring. Sometimes they made a frame of four sturdy twigs lashed together with basketry materials; the warp was strung vertically from the top to the bottom horizontal bar. Woven beadwork was used for headbands, armbands, scarfs, garters, and belts.

Beadwork and quillwork in the early periods of Indian life on the plains were functional and decorative, according to John C. Ewers in his pamphlet *Blackfeet Crafts*. He notes that Blackfeet women prided themselves on their skills as seamstresses, but, often piecing together two or more buffalo, elk, or antelope skins to form a shirt or dress resulted in joinings that could not be hidden by even the cleverest handwork. So the joinings were covered with bands of decoration in beadwork, quillwork, or ornamental skin fringe. Some researchers suggest that the reason for long decorative fringe on sleeves was to cover the long seam.

Beadwork has been an exciting craft used by the American Indian since the 1700s, when the tiny glass objects were traded for furs and skins. This detail of the panel used for a wall hanging 2 feet by 3 feet on page 177 shows a contemporary adaptation of seed-beading techniques with fabric appliqué. By Linda Jones.

American Indians were by no means the earliest or the only people to use beadwork extensively, although their designs are distinctive and a high achievement among their many crafts. Beads go back so far in history and have been so widely used all over the world that they must be recognized as some of the earliest and most meaningful of all human possessions. Some sculptures that predate written history have beads represented on them, though they have little other detail.

A brief survey of various cultures reveals that beads in many forms, shapes, and materials, but made mostly of glazed earthenware or stone, existed in the Minoan-Mycenaean and Egyptian cultures. In Ptolemaic and Roman periods, molded glass pendants were made with clay molds, many with facial images. The Oriental cultures had beads from earliest times. And primitive cultures in Africa and Oceania continue to use beads for ceremonial garments, as did their ancestors.

MATERIALS

You will need an assortment of beads in various sizes and colors and with holes of different diameters, depending on how many times the threads will be pulled through the beads. Use quilting thread, linen, waxed linen, or dental floss for stringing, depending upon the technique planned. Backing fabric should be stretched in a hoop or other frame; it can be felt, cotton, silk—anything you want to embellish with the glitter of beading. Use beading needles thin enough to fit through the hole of the bead and sharp enough to penetrate the base fabric.

Simplify work methods by separating the beads by size and color and by eliminating any inferior beads. Do not use misshapen or outsize beads; they will show up immediately in the finished project as an irregularity.

SEWN BEADWORK

The Single Bead Stitch uses one needle and thread. Draw a pattern line. Thread the needle and sew through the fabric. Beads may be placed together or far apart in regular or random arrangements. There will be as many stitches beneath the fabric as there are beads.

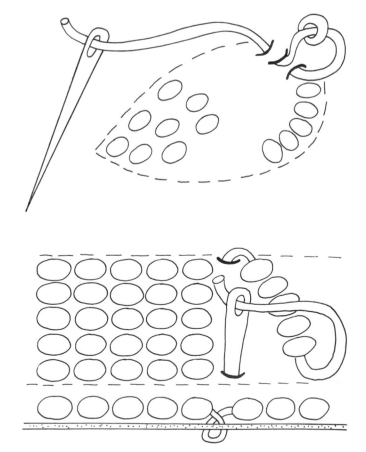

The Lazy Stitch is a quick, easy method for attaching rows of beads strung close together. Several beads are strung on the needle and the needle is passed through the fabric. A short back stitch is taken; the needle is brought up to the surface and again threaded with the necessary number of beads. The rows may be placed close to one another or in any pattern desired.

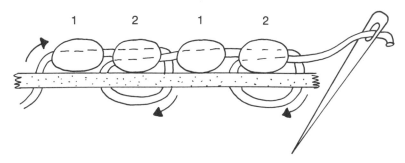

There are any number of progressions you can use to attach the beads with a single thread and make them firm and even. String two beads on your needle, insert the needle through the fabric, take a back stitch and reinsert the needle through the second bead as shown. Continue beading pairs and restringing through the second bead.

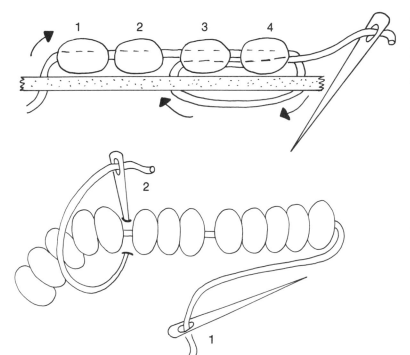

The same principle can be accomplished with four beads or any number desired. String the beads, insert the needle through the fabric, backstitch the width of two beads, bring the needle up and through beads 3 and 4, then string on another set of four beads and repeat.

COUCHING

To couch a length of beads to a surface, use two needles and two threads. String the beads on one needle and thread. Use the second length of thread to adhere the beaded length to the backing. Sew over the beaded thread every few beads depending upon the pattern desired.

Beaded pineapple shapes on a purse from Hong Kong and a floral shape with scattered beads decorate a glove from Italy. All use the Single Bead Stitch, the Lazy Stitch with seed beads and tube beads. Some rows in the floral pattern are couched, especially where curves are made.

Collection, Dona Meilach

Beaded belt (detail) woven on a loom. By Dorothy Bucker.

WEAVING BEADS ON LOOMS

Loom beading is extremely popular today and very easy to do, though it takes time and patience. You can make your own loom or buy one ready-made. For a beautiful loom-woven piece it is important to select beads that are uniform in diameter and width. The principle of beading on a loom is similar to weaving with warp and weft. In beading, however, a row of threaded beads is placed so one bead is between each warp thread. The beads are strung on the weft thread and placed horizontally under the warp so one bead lies between each warp thread. The weft thread is then passed over the end warp and again threaded through all the beads from the top. The warp must be held taut and be evenly spaced.

Woven beading may be used in its entirety for necklaces, collars, belts, and so forth. You can make a beaded shape and appliqué it to a garment or you may use woven beaded portions with sewn detailing.

Warp the loom with strong thread. For long pieces use a doubled thread on each outer edge. You may want to weave a few unbeaded weft rows back and forth in an under-one, over-one weave to prevent the beaded rows from slipping up. Follow a graphed-out pattern if you like. Straight-sided shapes are usually more successful than rounded shapes. When adding new weft lengths, tie knots in the middle of the work and weave thread ends back through several beads and cut off. Do not make knots at edges or they will protrude and show.

Commercial beading looms may vary in design, but essentially they consist of a frame with notched ends for holding the warp taut and even. Rollers at each end enable you to move the work and make it longer than the distance between the frame ends.

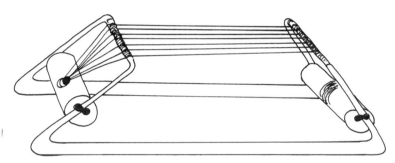

A handmade loom is usually a simple box or frame with two uprights notched to hold the warp; a nail at the center of each upright holds the warp ends. The loom should be 4 to 6 inches longer than the desired length of the finished item. The box or frame loom may be made as wide as you want the finished piece to be. Painting the loom a matte black will help reduce eye strain.

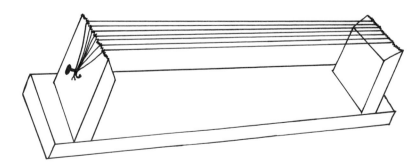

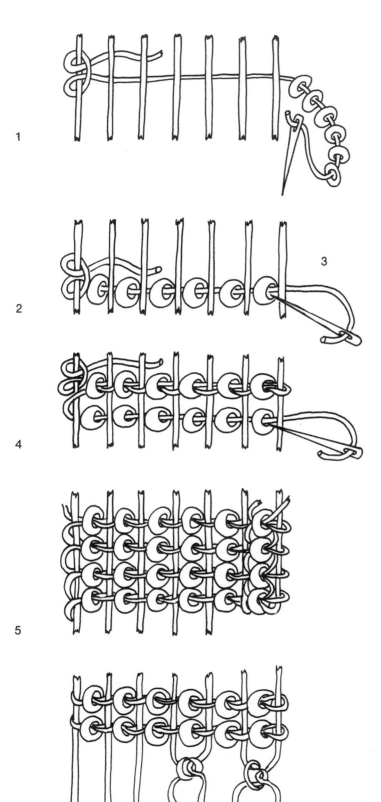

1. Attach the weaving thread to the left edge warp with a knot. Bring the thread under all the warp and string the necessary number of beads on the thread so there will be one bead between each warp (six beads for seven warp threads).

2. Hold the beads with your left forefinger. Place so one bead is between each warp.

3. Bring the weaving thread over the right edge warp and string it through all the beads toward the left and *over* all the warp. The first row is complete.

4. Bring your needle around the left-edge warp and *under* all the warp. String on a second row of beads and repeat the process.

5. When the weaving is completed, conceal the warp ends by threading one warp thread at a time onto a needle and working it back up through the rows of beads as shown.

6. Warp ends may be finished decoratively by Square Knotting, adding vertical lengths of beads, wrapping, or other treatments.

Couched beading in a floral design for a belt made by the Crow Indians. The rows of stitching on the back reflect the directions of the beading on the front.

Beaded knife sheaf with feathers made by Sioux Indians about 1870. Lazy Stitch.

The Zapotec Indians of Mexico excel in intricate hand beading.

All examples on this page photographed at San Diego Museum of Man

A Crow Indian necklace is characterized by rows of different-colored beads with additional beading worked around the animal claws.

Collection,
Field Museum of Natural History, Chicago

A loom-beaded necklace by Lee Erlin Snow.

Beaded amulets for umbilical cords are magical charms made by the Sioux Indians.

Photographed at
San Diego Museum of Man

A design drawn from the fretwork on a serpent's back and used in pre-Hispanic Mexico is adaptable to beadwork.

Beading couched on felt, then appliquéd to leather with additional beading and used for a purse panel. By Mandy Arrington.

A beaded bag by the Crow Indians.
Photographed at
San Diego Museum of Man

Beaded box top. By Jorjanna Lundgren.

Detail of a beaded blouse front. By Elisabeth Schimitschek.

Beaded Indian pouches showing the use of an interior couched design *(left)* and an overall pattern with the Lazy Stitch *(right)*.

Collection, Roger Brown, Chicago

Couched beading with wrapping on a stuffed leather neckband is combined with lengths of strung beads, liquid silver, and beach pebbles. By Lucia.
Collection, Dona Meilach

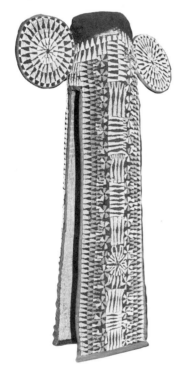

Secret Society mask of the Bamileke, Cameroon, Africa, is intricately patterned with beads in white and shades of blue. The beaded cloth mask is worn over a blue and white cotton robe.
Collection, Field Museum of Natural History, Chicago

Modern adaptations of American Indian beadwork are combined with wrapping and pendants on leather neckbands. By Lucia.

Linda Jones' woven beaded necklace. Pre-Hispanic design.

A halter made with seed and tube beads is used for a Middle Eastern belly dance costume. By Delilah.

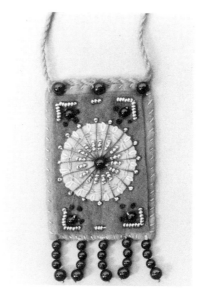

Pendant by Dee Menagh is made of felt appliqué with beading and embroidery.

A bracelet with beads strung on wire for the center section. By Mandy Arrington.

From top, reading clockwise:
Velvet and suede moccasin with couched beading by Linda Jones; woven necklace by Dorothy Bucker; Linda Jones' matching moccasin; deerskin with velvet moccasin and leather thong braiding around the edge by Berrylynn Freeby; leather moccasin with beaded velvet cuff by Elisabeth Schimitschek.

Sioux Indian leather moccasin (1905).
Photographed at
San Diego Museum of Man

Crow Indian beaded belt with repeat floral designs.
Photographed at
San Diego Museum of Man

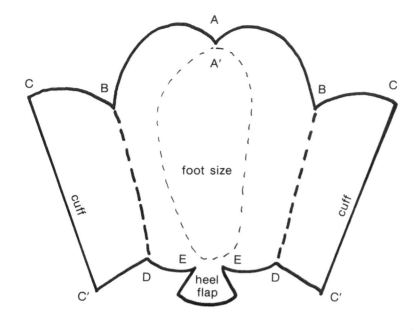

foot size

cuff

cuff

heel flap

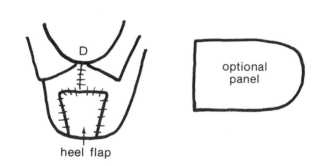

heel flap

optional panel

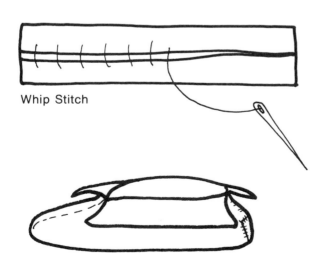

Whip Stitch

MAKING A MOCCASIN

You will need scrap fabric for making the pattern about 12 inches square, needle, and basting thread, two 12-inch squares (approximately) of soft leather, glover's needle (or any needle that will penetrate the leather), waxed linen, marking pen, beads for decorating.

MAKING THE PATTERN

1. Outline the shape of your foot on the scrap fabric but reshape the toe of the sole to a central point. A moccasin should fit snugly and may be worn on either foot; it stretches to fit as it is worn.
2. Allow one inch between A' and A from the center sole. Extend the pattern to point B on each side around the widest part of your foot. Make this shape wide enough so points B will meet across your top instep *plus* a ⅛-inch seam allowance.
3. Continue the pattern for the cuffs to points C and C'.
4. Continue the pattern to D and E and around for the heel flap *plus* ⅛-inch seam allowance.
5. Cut out the fabric pattern and baste together to be sure it fits, following the assembly instructions below. Then un-baste and transfer the pattern to the leather with the toe-to-heel length along the grain of the leather. Cut out the leather with a sharp scissors.
OPTIONAL: If you wish to add a beaded panel (as in the finished examples at left) plan a tonguelike leather shape to fit over the front seam. Bead the shape before assembling.

ASSEMBLING

All seams will be sewn on the outside with a waxed linen thread and a glover's needle.
1. Shape the leather around the sole. Bring points B together and gather seam A to B as you sew to form the toe and conform to the shape of your foot. Fold back the cuff.
2. Bring points D together and pull to fit the heel. Sew seam D to E with the heel flap on the outside.
3. Bring the heel flap up and sew over the back heel seam with a Whip Stitch.
4. Note: If you plan the optional beaded panel, assemble it by Whip Stitching it over the front toe seam *before* assembling the heel area.

TRIM

Beading toes and sides should be accomplished before assembling. Beading on cuffs can be done after assembly. Beading may be worked on velvet or other fabric, then appliquéd to the moccasin parts.

Ute Indian high-top side-buttoned moccasin. Each Indian tribe represents flowers and styles in slightly different forms, and these are the clues used by anthropologists for identifying them. The detail below can be used for your own beading projects.

Photographed at
San Diego Museum of Man

Use the beadwork drawings for developing original designs.

Enlarge this panel for a wall hanging in a large size or for an appliqué on a jacket in a smaller circle. Use portions only, if you prefer, for a handbag embellishment. By Linda Jones.

Bird design on the buckskin gauntlet by the Crow Indians.

*Photographed at
San Diego Museum of Man*

The back yoke of a jacket is beaded; an interesting placement by Berrylynn Freeby.

star   morning star

camp circle   mountains

arrow point   cloud

life   bear foot

parfleche   center

QUILLWORK

Quillwork is a uniquely American Indian craft which became practically obsolete in the 1880s when the popularity of beadwork put an end to the difficulty of using porcupine quills. Beads were easier to obtain, brighter in color, and more permanent. But quillwork deserves to be studied in the context of ethnic needlework because it can yield an excellent stimulus for new approaches. The story of porcupine quills used by the Plains Indians is fascinating. For those who are interested in re-creating Indian crafts, a few sources can supply quills similar to those used in the eighteenth and nineteenth centuries.

One porcupine yields about eight ounces of quills, which are so light in weight that there are about four thousand quills to the ounce. They vary in length from about one to twelve inches depending upon the animal and area of the country it comes from. The finest ones from the belly are about one inch long and very thin. The natural colored quills are whitish with black tips, but they were often colored with natural dyestuffs: commercial fabric dyes may be used today.

Before use, the quills were soaked in water, cut into thin strips, and flattened with a piece of bone. Some women softened them in their mouths and flattened them between their teeth. They were sewn to buckskin or other material in various ways; basically two parallel lengths of sinew (used as thread) were sewn through the leather at intervals and the quill folded under the thread between each stitch. The flattened quill appears as a series of short bands as in the bag, (detail opposite right). Variations resulted when the quills were bent at different angles or when the stitches were placed in different relationships before the quills were placed on them. Quillwork patterns were always geometric shapes with horizontal and vertical bands. Some quills were plaited and woven between the threads. Some tribes wrapped them around a single thread.

Quillwork was used for the same purposes as beading—it appeared on bands of fabric covering seams, on cuffs, vests, leggings, gauntlets, and all other Indian garments and accessories. Some quillwork was done on birchbark shaped into boxes.

"Contemporary quillwork" will usually not involve real porcupine quills. Rather, the designs will be emulated in more readily available materials such as plastic tubing and plastic straws, ordinary broom straw, and cut lengths of rattan and colored beads. The quillwork designs, which were the basis of much beadwork by the Indians, are marvelously adaptable to today's ethnic trends. If you use clear plastic tubing, as in the examples by B. J. Adams on the following pages, color can be achieved by stitching colored yarn through the tubing and to the ground fabric. Other materials can be glued to fabrics and hard surfaces.

Designs used for quillwork and beading by the Blackfeet Indians were symbols.

The shapes in a star pattern are colored and flattened porcupine quills in this detail of a Cheyenne Indian clothes bag.
Collection,
Field Museum of Natural History, Chicago

Below:
Left: A Comanche painted rawhide bag could be interpreted in beadwork, appliqué, embroidery, or other needlework techniques in combination with one another.
Center: The design on a Blackfeet bag in quillwork looks like a modern necklace pattern.
Right: The Dakota design uses several repeat geometric shapes within one another and in different sizes.

front view

back view

Sioux-doe quill body ornament (front and back views) by B. J. Adams. Industrial clear plastic tubing with colored yarns on black fabric. Detail of collar, *opposite page*. The tubing is cut in lengths and stitched to the surface, as is beadwork. A preliminary pattern made to the actual size of the adornment was sketched on graph paper. The tubes were cut to necessary lengths and laid out on the paper. The design was transferred to the fabric and the tubes sewn in place. The tubing for the fringe is of a smaller diameter than that of the larger designs and is held in place with clear monofilament rather than colored yarn.

Photos, Clark Adams

The collar shape is pseudo-Egyptian although embellished with the geometric shapes of Indian quillwork.

In progress: Basting stitches indicate the placement of the tubing. The coloring was worked out carefully in colored pencils before actual colored yarns and tubing were stitched to the ornament.

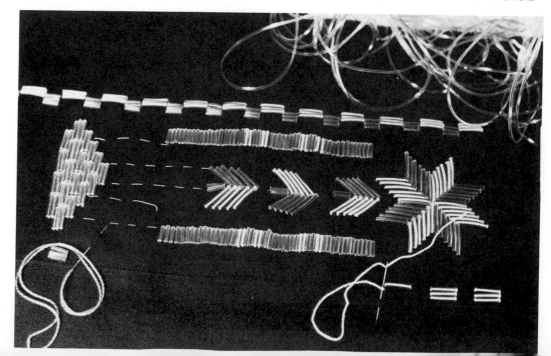

9. Gathering and Smocking

AMONG THE ENCHANTING ASPECTS OF MOVIES BASED ON LIFE IN England in the 1800s are the smocks worn by the country people. The smock, a loose-fitting garment with ornamental gathers at the top, was often elaborately and beautifully embroidered. Most workers had everyday and "Sunday best" smocks that differed from one another in the materials and the amount of detailing.

The actual meaning of the word "smock" in old English was "shift" or "chemise," which Webster now lists as archaic. The current definition is "a light loose garment especially for protection of clothing while working." The word "smocking" has remained, however, and is commonly used to describe the detailing on garments other than the English smock. The same type of gathering is found in many cultures where the peasant garb needed to be roomy for comfort and air circulation while the top around the shoulder and chest had to fit the body neatly.

One historian notes that royalty liked the dress design and cites costumes worn by Mary Tudor of the English royal family, "who was Spanish in all her tastes and had smocks all worked in Spanish stitches, black and gold or black silk only. This taste, following the political tendencies of the times, disappeared under Elizabeth." It is interesting to observe that it did survive in the Low Countries in peasant dress. The Spanish aspect continues to appear extensively in blouses and dresses of Spain and Mexico.

Smocking serves the purpose of holding fabric together in neat tiny pleats. It is perfect on any garment where fullness has to be controlled, for example, on children's dresses, lingerie, and of course, ethnic styles. Once the pleating is accomplished, the folds, sometimes called tubes, may be embroidered with a variety of stitches and other embellishments.

Pleats are always made in the fabric before the parts are sewn together. A smocked detail made on a separate piece of fabric can be overlaid onto another portion of a garment.

All smocking begins the same way. Parallel threads are run through the fabric and pulled to form tiny pleats. The number of stitches and rows and the distances between the threads determine the density of the smocking. The density can range from a simple free pleating used on a cuff or neckline to the thoroughly smocked bodice and sleeves on Pat Wheeler's contemporary rendition of the English smock (left). Smocking and gathering are used in several of the patterns shown in Chapter 13; but they may be worked into any pattern where you think they would be practical and wonderful.

Pat Wheeler based her individualized smock on the design and ideas of a nineteenth-century English peasant smock. Decorations in those days were symbols denoting a person's occupation. Pat loves to garden, so she embroidered gardener's symbols.

183

MAKING THE GATHERS

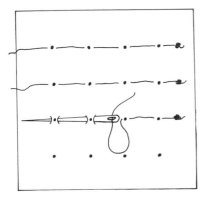

The fabric is marked with dots ironed onto the wrong side from a transfer. Begin by inserting the needle under the first right-hand dot on the wrong side of the fabric. Place a knot at the thread end, then take very regular stitches in a straight line along the weft of the material, picking up each dot along the line. Leave a few inches of thread hanging loose at the end of the row. Work the next row of dots the same way until all the rows are stitched.

Pull the fabric evenly along the threads until the pleat density desired is achieved and all the folds are even. Tie off the gathering-threads in pairs so the pleats do not pull out. Gathering-threads are removed when the decoration is completed. The pleated area is now ready for embroidery.

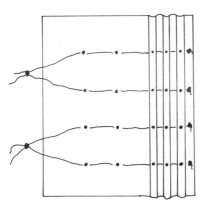

MATERIALS FOR SMOCKING AND GATHERING

Smooth and even textured fabrics such as cotton, silk, linen, fine wools, and permanent-press materials are ideal for smocking. Finer fabrics such as voiles and thin silks are beautiful but require more patience and practice. Heavy materials are usually too bulky. Generally, figure that fabric, before smocking, should measure about three times the finished dimension desired. This will vary depending upon how far apart the stitches are made and the density of the pleating. There are transfers available with dots equidistant so that all your stitches and the resulting pleats are even. These are pressed onto the back of the fabric. Transfers with dots about ¼ to ⅜ inch apart are suitable for most fabrics. Initial stitching can be done by hand or with a special foot on a sewing machine.

Embroidery cotton and perle cotton are sturdy threads for smocking; other threads can be used for the applied embroidery.

Designs from Coptic textiles are perfect for smocking embroidery.

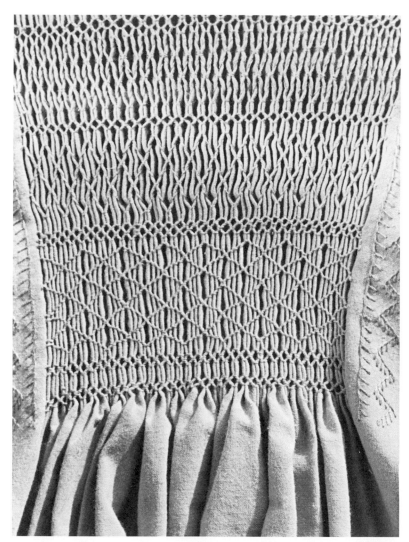

SMOCKING STITCHES

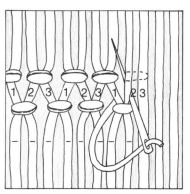

The Honeycomb Stitch is a double backstitch made over two pleats which alternate every row. Mark the rows. Work from left to right. Bring the needle out to the left of pleat 1. Take two backstitches over pleats 1 and 2; bring the needle up and out to the left of pleat 2. Make two backstitches over pleats 2 and 3. Bring the needle down and out to the left of pleat 3 for the next stitch.

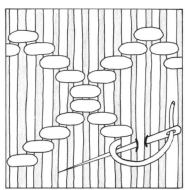

The Trellis Stitch is a single backstitch worked over two pleats at a time in a zigzag pattern. The needle is inserted under one pleat with the thread over the needle.

Both stitches are shown in the smocked garment details at left by Pat Wheeler. The smocking was accomplished on a rectangular shape of material, then inserted between the side panels. The side panels are embroidered with motifs that match those on the smocking.

Smocking is embroidered with blue and white figures. The panel is the front for a dress richly embroidered with flowers and joined with lace inserts. Zapotec Indian, Oaxaca, Mexico.

Pleating and gathering with machine embroidery. Mixe Indian, Mexico. Pleating and gathering do not stretch; smocking has elasticity.

Pleating with smocking and a gathered ruffle. Zapotec Indian, Oaxaca, Mexico.

All examples this page:
San Diego Museum of Man

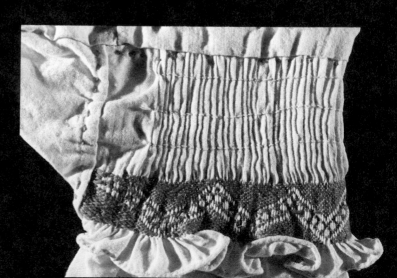

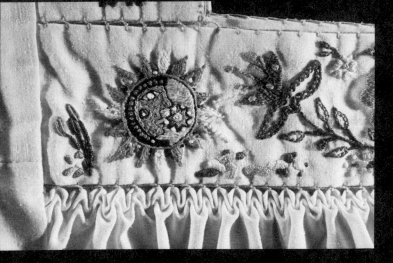

Linda Jones emulated a blouse made by the Mixe Indians of Mexico. A hand-embroidered panel is assembled to the smocked and shoulder panels with fagoting and openwork stitches (see page 223, Chapter 12).

Detail of an unusual and characteristic stitch used by the Zapotec Indians of Mexico. The embroidery thread is caught under the peak of the pleat when stitching. The unstitched pleats become the exposed design.

A gathered and smocked Mexican blouse embroidered with Cross Stitching.

Collection, Mimi Levinson

An Oriental hat with pleating.

Opposite page:
Three versions of a Roumanian blouse with options of pleating, gathering, or smocking for the neckline and sleeves. Folkwear Pattern No. 103. (See Chapter 13 for additional patterns.)
Courtesy, Folkwear
Photo, Jerry Wainwright

The contemporary Greek costume appears to be derived from those of the ancients in the use of a fully pleated skirt and sleeves.

The placement of pleats and gathers in costumes from early Grecian clothing that is pictured on vases and other artifacts can offer ideas for contemporary needlework. Observe the location of the pleats and the use of designs that can be copied in embroidery.

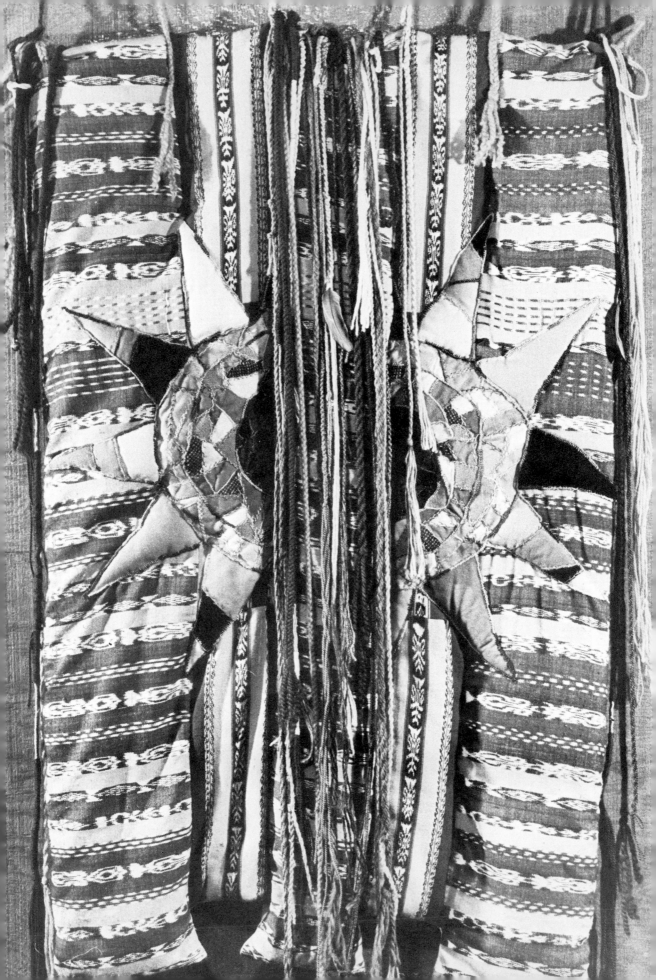

10. Dimensional Soft Work

SUNSPLIT. Jorjanna Lundgren. A kaleidoscope of cultural inspirations resulted in a wall hanging with a symbolic stylized sun appliquéd onto a multicolored background. Cascading elements give a rough, tribal appearance. Traditional techniques include patchwork with quilting for the dimensional presentation.

DIMENSIONAL SOFT WORK TAKES ITS CUE FROM PADDED NEEDLE-work used by many cultures throughout time. The most obvious derivation would be quilting and trapunto. We tend first to think of the quilts made in England and in America during the past century. And they serve as an excellent point of departure for contemporary soft work in new styling and dimensions.

Quilting, the process of making padded materials for warmth from two or three layers of material, has many approaches other than the patterned and patchwork quilts of early Americana that we so readily associate with it. In fact, some of the terms we now use to describe quilting procedures are quite new and have appeared only in the past fifty to sixty years. Essentially, they are:

English or American quilting, before it became popular in our vernacular, was referred to as "wadding quilting," and the filler material was the same size as the layers; all three were held together by sewing. The quilts were used mostly for warmth on beds.

Italian quilting was referred to as "cord" or "corded quilting." It is easily recognizable because parallel lines, or other linear patterns, are raised against a flat fabric background. Italian quilting consists of two layers of material placed together with lengths of cording sewn between the layers to achieve the pattern.

191

A padded hat has a quilted section stitched to create triangle designs. Versions of this hat are found throughout Oriental cultures.

Trapunto, in fourteenth-century Italy, where it probably originated, was called "stuffed quilting." Two layers of fabric are used, but the design is not restricted to parallel lines. The lining fabric is slit and padding is placed within the materials to make any kind of design. The backing fabric is then stitched up by hand.

Origins of padded work are believed to date back as far as 3400 B.C. Averil Colby, in his book *Quilting,* observed that small ivory figures in the British Museum wear "a cloak or mantle, on which the carved patterns are characteristic of a quilted textile. The garment hangs stiffly and not in the soft folds of a single thickness of material." In his book, Colby stated that the authors of *Needlework Through the Ages* believe the carving on a First Dynasty Egyptian king's garment shows his apparel as faithfully as other carved representations of the time: "The pattern is carved in deep relief and does not suggest a surface decoration of applied or embroidered thread—it is more likely that...the raised character of the carved pattern produces an effect identical with that of quilting over a soft yielding substance like wool or down....This robe might have been designed for a ceremony at which white only was permitted and this would add strength to the quilting theory."

Early American patterns are re-created on a large tablelike quilting frame. Designs are drawn on the fabric, which is laid over a padded filler and muslin backing. The stitching is accomplished through all three layers. The result is decorative and useful for its warmth.

Quilted jackets used for warmth appear in illustrations of objects in early Oriental cultures and almost every country where temperatures are frigid. Historical records, drawings, and paintings indicate that quilting was used in the construction of defensive body armor in the Middle Ages. "Armor," sometimes made of quilted leather, linen, or similar fabrics rather than metals, had several advantages. The padded thickness was reasonable defense against the cut and thrust of the sword, the spear, or the arrow; it became useless only in the face of cannon shot or pistols. Fabric armor, compared to metal, was lighter and less cumbersome on long marches, easier to put on and take off, and less costly to make.

Quilted armor is often referred to by Geoffrey Chaucer (1340–1400) in his *Canterbury Tales.* In Edmund Spenser's late-sixteenth-century epic poem *The Faerie Queene,* several descriptions of quilted garments appear.

The direction of this chapter is to note the rich historical background of padded work and to shift your visual and mental gears to apply the techniques to fashionable clothing and decorations. Here you will find traditional quilting methods explored, then applied to forms you may not have thought of. You will discover combinations of English quilting and trapunto, and even patchwork quilting, dissociated from its usual function. Various embellishments already illustrated in other chapters are added to the dimensional soft work used for clothing, wall hangings, jewelry, and sculpture in relief and in three dimensions.

Where can you seek ideas for thinking of quilting dimensionally? We suggest you look in travel books, museum publications, and magazines such as the *National Geographic,* to spark ethnic adaptations. For example, you may see a wrapped headband and belt on a Nigerian woman; it can initiate a new set of thought processes. Ask yourself, "How can I interpret that woman's garment into something practical or an updated fashion? How do the shapes and colors of the prints relate? Using one or more images for inspiration, could I make a hat? a cummerbund? a jacket? or a sculpture? What technique would be best?" Your experiences and thought processes will lead you to creative new statements—and no two people looking at the same photo will evolve identical answers.

You can jog your thinking in another direction, too. Observe a tribal mask or a carving such as the Maprik River ceremonial figure at right. The entire face could become the inspiration for a stuffed wall hanging as in the piece on page 207 by Marilla Argüelles. Perhaps only a detail of the painted design on the head or hip, the chest or chin, could suggest a border design for a neckline or cuff that could be lightly stuffed. Kachina dolls, totem pole carvings, and other illustrations throughout the book can be used for quilting ideas, also.

Carry your thinking further along exotic routes and incorporate tassels, beading, metal threads, and mirrors in your padded pieces. The more you observe in photos and in the costumes of people as you travel and attend dances or theatre where ethnic costumes are worn, the more you can sharpen your interests and appreciation for the variety that exists.

With this background, stuffed needlework becomes another tool you can employ to create the artistic images you visualize.

Designs adaptable to padded work may be gleaned from entire pieces or from small details of wood sculptures such as this painted ceremonial figure from the Maprik River area of New Guinea.
Courtesy, Field Museum of Natural History, Chicago

A quilting frame for small projects is an enlarged version of an embroidery hoop that is attached to a floor stand.

MATERIALS AND METHODS FOR QUILTING

The fabrics you select for dimensional soft work will be dictated by the project. If you plan to work in a quilting method, you will probably find a closely woven material such as linen, silk, satin, velvet, or a synthetic fabric most suitable. Muslin may be used for backing fabric. It is also necessary to determine how much wear and washings the item will take. A quilt or jacket to be used for warmth will be subject to cleaning more often than a mask used for a wall hanging. When determining amounts of fabric needed, always allow for hems. For a patchwork-quilted surface, the patches should each have a ¼-inch seam allowance. All design pieces to be appliquéd should be ironed flat and smooth.

Where practical, the enlarged design can be transferred to the top fabric with dressmaker's carbon and a carbon wheel. If the pattern is too intricate to trace off readily, enlarge the design on sections of wrapping paper to the size the finished object will be. Place the paper in your sewing machine and, with an unthreaded needle, machine stitch along the design lines to produce perforated holes. Then place this perforated paper pattern on your fabric and rub stamping powder or tailor's chalk through the holes. Be sure to place the design so it will work out with the proper side up if it is not symmetrical. Run a basting stitch or chalk line along the perforated powder so you can see it clearly.

Assemble the layers of fabric padding and backing as necessary. Pin, then baste them together along both the crosswise and lengthwise grains of the fabric.

Filler Padding

The thickness and method of padding must also be dictated by the project. The sewing counters of your fabric supplier will have a selection. Remember, the heavier the padding the warmer the object and coarser the stitching will be. With thinner padding, the quilting stitches will be finer and closer together. You will find a selection of thick- and thin-layered cotton and Dacron batting and polyester fiber fill. For many projects, such as soft purses, vests, portions of garments, and relief wall hangings, new or used flannel and cotton mattress-pad materials are easy and practical fillers. Mattress padding is already stitched and will not shift during the quilting procedures as some of the more loosely composed fiber fills tend to do. You may also use sheets of foam rubber cut to shape and size needed. Even disposable baby diapers can be used for small areas.

Commercially prequilted fabrics, available as yard goods in carefully chosen prints and solids, can be combined for a variety of effects that would echo the origins of many cultures. It is possible to short-cut the quilting process by using portions of prequilted materials, then perhaps adding your own border designs, appliqué, embroidery, and other detailing for individualized clothing and accessories.

Sewing

Quilting may be accomplished on a sewing machine or by hand. Machine quilting can be done with or without a quilting foot. For machine work, use a straight stitch with a stitch length of six to twelve per inch depending upon the material and filler. Cotton batting can be stitched with lines about two inches apart; Dacron with lines not more than three inches apart. Scroll and floral designs can be more easily followed with the short open toe of the quilting foot attachment.

For hand stitching, stretching the materials in a hoop or frame will facilitate the work. When a frame is not available, place the materials on a table or in your lap and work small portions at a time. Use a short, even Running Stitch, a sturdy single thread between Nos. 30 and 50 with a sharp No. 8 or 9 needle. A special 100 percent cotton quilting thread with a glazed finish is available.

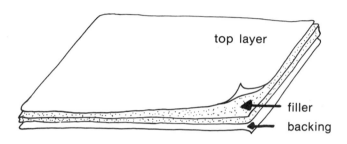

top layer

filler

backing

Place three layers together along both the crosswise and lengthwise grain of the fabric:

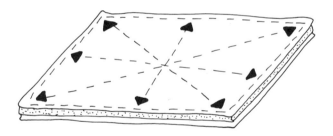

Baste. Begin at the center and work outward. Use a running stitch that penetrates all three layers. By beginning at the center, the padding lies smoothly and the layers will not tend to pucker. Always work extra fullness to the edge. Sew in the same progression, cutting the basting thread as necessary. As you work closer to the outer edges, use smaller embroidery hoops. Cut away any excess filler before hemming.

Each stitch and interval should be of equal length for best results.

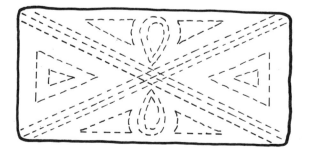

A sample pattern of a quilted design could be used on the front of a garment; portions could be elongated or repeated for borders and cuffs.

Detail of stuffed appliqué by Joan Michaels Paque.

RAISED QUILTED SHAPES

Trapunto, or stuffed quilting, and Italian quilting depend on a filler material being added in portions of the design for the effect rather than an overall padding and stitching. The placement of the padding gives a relief, or raised, design on some portions of the fabric; it may be regular cording lines or abstract shapes. The stuffed portions are stitched close; a lining may or may not be used, depending upon the project. As these techniques and their use have been adopted, different authors term them differently. The exact names of the methods are not so important as how you use them in your individual creations.

THE HAWAIIAN QUILT

The stylized designs and appliqué methods characteristic of Hawaiian quilts can be adapted to other needlework projects. They are elegant for skirts. Try smaller patterning for purses or perhaps for portions or details for jackets. The breadfruit tree, pineapple, and other flowers and plants have become traditional with individualized variations. The top surface of

English padding: The bottom layer of fabric is slit, stuffed, then sewn together with a Whip Stitch. The padding shows on the right side of the quilted layers.

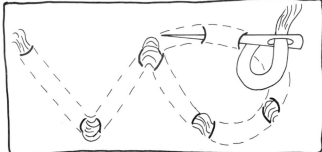

Trapunto or corded quilting: A ¼-inch linear design is formed with Running Stitches. The underside of the fabric is slit horizontally across the linear design every few inches. A cord is passed through the line using a blunt needle.

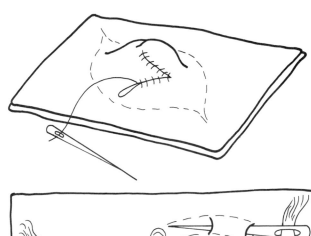

Padded quilted areas may also be created by adding shapes on the underside of the fabrics. Pieces are pinned into place and stuffed from one edge with kapok or other material. Then the area is sewn. In the previous techniques the design is stitched first, then stuffed.

the quilt is appliquéd with cutout fabrics in one, two, or three bold solid colors. The stitches usually follow the contours of the appliqué using straight, shell-like or wavelike lines one to two inches apart.

The techniques of trapunto and quilting, in themselves derived from other cultures, may be applied to a variety of individualized expressive sculptural forms and wall hangings. In recent years, such forms have been called "soft sculpture" and have earned their place in many gallery and museum shows alongside more traditional sculptural media.

Padded, stitched materials have an inherent surface dimension. By manipulating them they can be worked into dimensional objects. When heavy fabrics are used, the materials become stiff and readily shapeable. Thinking of sculptural dimensional form requires consideration of the external shape of the object and its relation to the space it occupies in addition to the design on the two-dimensional surfaces. Such pieces can be created in solid fabrics, in preprinted fabrics, in appliqué, and in materials that are hand-dyed by painting and/or batiking.

a. Sara Santos cut the pattern of heavy paper; her design is based on a version of the carnation. The cut-paper designs are pinned onto eight layers of folded fabric; the straight edge of the paper is placed on the fold and along the bias.

b. When the cut fabric is unfolded, it is strung out on the top layer of the quilt material. The fabric is cut much like a string of paper dolls.

a

b

c

d

c. The pattern pieces are pinned, then basted, working from the center of the quilt to the outside. Then the appliqué is stitched to the top fabric. Finally, the top fabric, filler, and lining are assembled and the entire design is stitched.

d. Detail of a finished quilt by Sara Santos. The regular Running Stitches follow the contour of the flower on both the appliqué and the background.

The Turkish coat with vertical printed stripes at the right in the photograph on the opposite page served as pattern and inspiration for a contemporary version designed by Folkwear. The modernized coat is quilted and reversible with a diamond-shaped trapunto border made by hand or machine. The pattern offers six variations for materials, techniques, and combinations.

Above: Detail of the trapunto patterns.
Courtesy, Folkwear
Photos, Jerry Wainwright

Opposite page:
Cate Fitt's individualized adaptation of the Folkwear Turkish coat *(previous page)* is made of hand-dyed and -painted silks with intricate quilting patterns in geometric and stylized designs. (See color pages.)

Mandala jacket by Marilla Argüelles combines patchwork, appliqué, and quilting. The jacket was made from a Vogue pattern. The mandala was inspired by the cover of the book *Tantric Mysticism of Tibet* by John Blofeld.

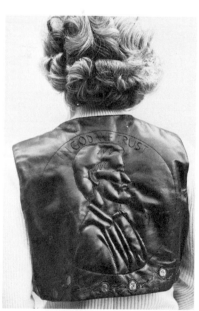

Carol Lockwood used an American penny as the design source for the vest back in English quilting on leather. Coins, held in place with the same embroidery stitches used to hold shi sha mirrors, outline the vest back and are carried through to the front.

A Manchurian-style jacket by Gisela Dennert is made of machine-quilted hand-batiked cotton velvet.

Cloisonné enamels of the Byzantine cultures inspired B. J. Adams' stuffed beads made of satin with hand- and machine-stitched metallic threads and perle cotton. The polyester-stuffed beads are alternated with red wooden beads. The neck tube is made of ribbons sewn together and cut on the diagonal.

Photo, Clark Adams

The Benin altar head *(below)* could serve as inspiration for the soft chocker by Lou Ann Forbes made of three tubes of colored stuffed jersey embellished with American Indian buttons and Egyptian paste beads.

By Pattie Frazer. A neck trim in batik fabric has been worked in the trapunto technique. A matching border on each cuff is hand-painted but not padded.

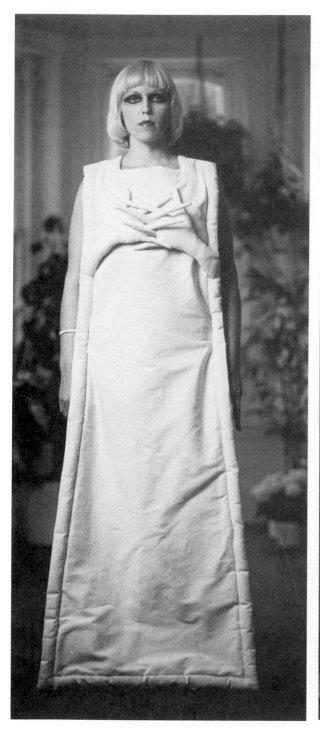

John Harris carried the contemporary stuffing theme further in a gown titled "Caress" made of cotton canvas with a cotton gauze coat.

Courtesy, artist

Left:
A basic tunic pattern has a novel adaptation of trapunto. Titled "Folded Hands," it is made of cotton canvas. By John Harris.

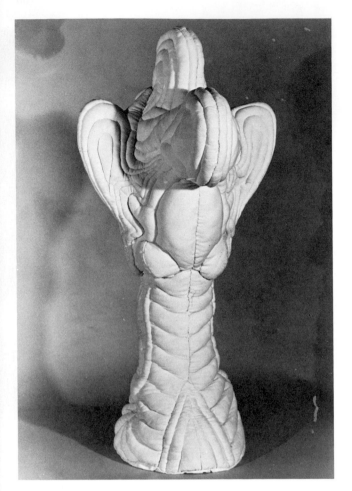

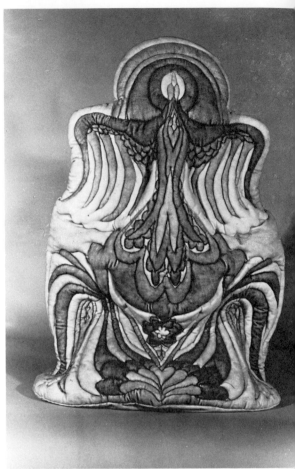

Two velveteen sculptures by Jacqueline Snyders of trapunto and stuffing techniques. The form *(left)* is white velveteen and stands 31 inches high, 17 inches wide, and 15 inches deep. At right, the dye-painted velveteen "Fairytale Fantasy" is 24 inches high, 16 inches wide, and 10 inches deep.

Courtesy, artist

The East Indian influence is apparent in the detailing of a soft padded box by Tony Prescott. She crumple-tie-dyed cloth with brilliant purples, blues, and lavenders. The cloth was cut to fit a box, then padded and hand-sewn around the outside and inside. Many types of embroidery stitches are used with shi sha mirrors and tassels.

A design from an early northern French fabric was reinterpreted by Wende Cragg in an appliqué and quilted wall hanging. Rich blue velvets and velveteens are padded and machine-appliquéd. Some hand embroidery is used for detailing.

Courtesy, artist

A basically trapunto sculpture is embellished with lace trims, assorted embroidery stitches, and wrapped elements that hang down and away from the solid portion of the form. By Twyla Cottrell.

African wedding doll from the Turkana tribe (front and back views). Materials are leather, wood, beads, shells, and an old zipper (open and falling down either side of the figure).
Collection, Steve and Susan Nelson, Palos Verdes Estates, California

Contemporary fetish figure inspired by the Benin tribe of Africa. Woven body of wool with embellishments of metal, shell, beads, fur feathers, and a zipper influenced by the Turkana piece. By Susan Nelson.

Peruvian "mummy" boat. Such figures were made with many layers of cloth, and gifts within, then wrapped into a bundle. They were added to the burial shrouds; those that have been found in ancient cemeteries were preserved by the hot dry atmosphere and the desert sun. This piece probably dates from about 400 B.C.
Collection, Steve and Susan Nelson, Palos Verdes Estates, California

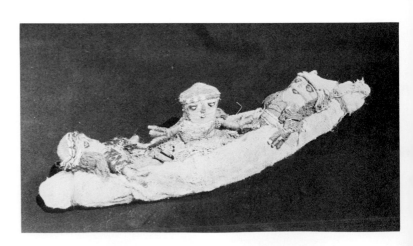

Fabric mask by Marilla Argüelles is taken from a New Guinea mask design. Maroon and black linen are appliquéd to a white linen backing. The padded and shaped face is mounted onto a wood backing. The hair is raffia with sisal rope at the "ears." The mask is 39 inches high, 25 inches wide.

11. Crochet

CONSIDERING THE LENGTH OF TIME THAT CROCHET HAS BEEN used by various European countries, it is surprising that there is no record of its having been used by any tribal cultures. Crochet, commonly associated with a hooked-tip needle, may also be accomplished with the fingers and with a straight needle. Researchers believe that crochet may have been used at the time of Jesus, but considering the perishability of fabrics and the fact that few historians have delved into the construction of garments in previous ages, it is difficult to pinpoint its existence in time.

The word "crochet" is derived from the French "croches," or "croc," and the old Danish "krooke," meaning hook. It was most often practiced in the nunneries in Europe during the sixteenth century and loosely categorized as nun's work for making lace. Crochet is believed to have been brought into Ireland at an early date and became known as "Irish Point" with patterns reminiscent of needle lace. In 1838 it attained more interest with the appearance of printed patterns and the manufacture of cotton threads. During the famines in Ireland in the mid-1840s, the crochet hook is credited with saving thousands of Irish people from starvation. The Irish nuns, searching for a way to teach the people to help themselves, taught crochet. When one industrious woman switched from knitting to crochet, orders poured in for this new look. She taught the craft to hundreds of other people and the technique quickly caught on. Crochet zoomed and became commercially important. Women who made crocheted laces, tablecloths, edges for linens, and clothing items turned their economy into a prosperous one.

Crochet soon spread to the continent and across the Atlantic to America when many of the Spanish immigrants crossed to the fertile land. It has been taught by missionaries to many nimble-fingered people in other countries but apparently it never sparked an indigenous style. Irish or Belgium lace produced by a woman in El Salvador or Africa still looks like Irish or Belgium lace. Crochet is used for edging blouses in Mexico, Guatemala, and the Philippines. In West Pakistan, shoes often have a chain-stitched edging that resembles crochet, but it is attached to the leather with an awl and worked with a straight needle rather than a hook.

Lillian Bryce cleverly combined woven squares with crochet. It is a contemporary adaptation of African kenté cloth, in which narrow woven strips are assembled. Additional panels and fringe were added onto the front and back of an old envelope-style purse, and it became a fresh, new accessory.

Crochet is an adaptable method for interpreting ethnic ideas in contemporary styling, as the following examples will verify. It lends itself to fine detail when it is worked with fine hooks and threads, or to rough, gutsy work when it is used with thick needles, heavy threads, and novelty yarns. The beauty of contemporary crochet is that once you learn the basic Chain Stitch and its variations, you can create shapes in very abstract manners to use as clothing embellishments and sculpture. For clothing, you can work crochet pieces to the same patterns that you use for cutting fabrics, then assemble them as you would fabric pieces. If you prefer to work from patterns, you can adapt those available in knitting and crochet instruction books by altering the colors, yarns, shaping, and embellishments as you like, to yield an exotic look.

Crochet hooks and materials are varied: hooks may be made of steel, wood, bone, or plastic; threads may be fine silks, novelty yarns, heavy jutes, wool, synthetics, and so forth. Crocheted lace squares by Sophie Smith. Wood carved hooks by Andi Dalton and Bill Dungan.

Kenté cloth made by the Ashanti of Africa is woven in narrow strips with designs added during the weaving procedure. The narrow strips are assembled and gussets set in. They were the inspiration for Lillian Bryce's use of squares assembled with crochet on page 255. The patterns could readily be added to garments with surface embroidery.
Collection, Dona Meilach

The versatility of assembled woven squares is evident in a dress by Lillian Bryce. The squares assembled with crochet form the dress front and back. The side gusset is an elongated triangle of crochet with squares inset. Detail at left.

The loom for weaving squares is available in craft shops. Squares may be only 4 by 4 inches. Some looms may be adjusted to make larger squares.

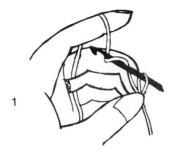

1

CROCHET

All crochet begins with a simple chain accomplished with a plastic, wood, or metal crochet hook. Large crochet loops can be made using your fingers as the hook, and this is often referred to as "finger crochet."

2

CROCHET CHAIN

1. Place a slipknot on hook held with the point toward you, as you would hold a pencil. Hold yarn in the other hand over your ring finger, under middle and over index finger, loosely enough so the yarn feeds smoothly as the hook pulls it.

2. Pass hook under and over yarn and draw it through the loop on the hook for as many stitches as you want the chain to be.

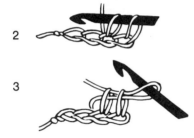

1

2

3

Single Crochet

1. Insert hook under two top strands of second stitch from hook. *For all crochet, hook is always inserted under both top loops* unless a different motif is desired.

2. Pass hook under and over yarn and draw it through the stitch to give you two loops on the hook.

3. Pass hook under and over yarn again and draw it through the two loops.

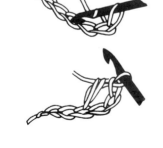

1

2

Half Double Crochet

1. Pass hook under and over yarn, insert hook into third stitch from hook.

2. Pass hook under and over yarn and draw it through stitch. Pass hook under and over yarn again and draw it through the three loops on the hook.

1

2

Double Crochet

1. Pass hook under and over yarn, insert hook into the fourth stitch from hook.

2. Pass hook under and over yarn and draw it through the stitch. Pass hook under and over yarn again. Draw yarn through the first two loops only on the hook. Pass hook under and over yarn again and draw it through the remaining two loops on hook.

Triple Crochet

1. Pass hook under and over yarn twice. Insert hook into the fifth stitch from hook.

2. Pass hook under and over yarn and draw it through the stitch. *Pass hook under and over yarn and draw through two loops, repeat from * twice.

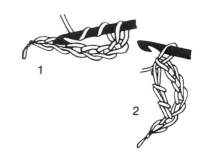

Increasing

Increasing is simple. You work two of whatever stitch you are doing anywhere in the row or at the end. Increasing is usually done with a single or double crochet.

Decreasing

Decrease can be made at any point and is usually done in a single or double crochet; each one is slightly different.

To Decrease in Single Crochet
1. Insert hook in stitch next to loop and draw yarn through (two loops on hook), insert hook in next stitch and draw yarn through (three loops on hook).

2. Pass hook under and over yarn and draw through all three loops. You actually work two stitches together to give a decrease of one.

To Decrease in Double Crochet
1. Pass hook under and over yarn, insert hook in next stitch and draw yarn through. There are three loops on hook.
2. Pass hook under and over and draw through two loops with two remaining on hook. Hook under and over yarn again.
3. Insert hook in next stitch and draw yarn through; four loops on hook.
4. Catch yarn again and draw through two loops; three loops remain on hook.
5. Catch yarn and draw through the three loops. A decrease of one double crochet is completed.

Ending: Simply pull the end of the thread through the last loops and remove hook.

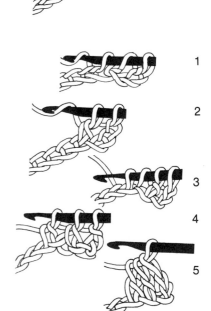

To Form a Circle
1. Make a chain of any number of stitches. Insert hook in first chain made. Catch yarn with hook. Be sure chain is not twisted.
2. Draw yarn through *both* the chain and the loop on hook. This is a "slip stitch," which can be used for any kind of joining. You now have a circle that can be expanded to any size you like using the same number of stitches to form a straight tubular crochet; or it can be shaped by increasing and decreasing.

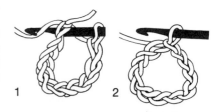

Crocheted jute is developed as a casual shoulder bag with an ethnic look. Wooden beads and driftwood complement the natural color and texture of the jute. By Twyla Cottrell.

A beaded Arapaho Indian clothes bag could be the inspiration for a contemporary purse.
Collection,
Field Museum of Natural History, Chicago

A Cheyenne Indian traveling bag offers shape ideas for a crocheted purse. The materials used are leather, porcupine quills and beading, and surface designing. You may interpret these in your own color and material combinations.
Collection,
Field Museum of Natural History, Chicago

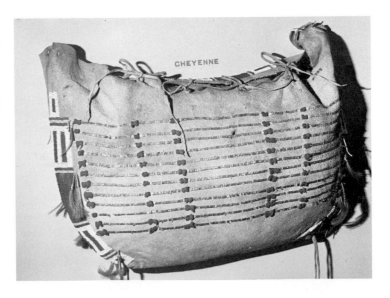

A handmade denim twill bag is combined with crocheted panels and a flap, that is loaded with crocheted goodies that give it an ethnic feeling. Multicolored wools in flat and raised crochet stitches have bells, tassels, and curlicues attached. By Vini Sozzani.

Actually Mandy Arrington used an East Indian shoulder bag for her design inspiration. The leather bag is free-style crochet, with crochet curlicues and a braided leather handle. Front (*left*) and back (*below*) are different.

LADY AND THE ZEPHYR LILIES. Jacqueline Snyders. Crocheted wool and mohair wall hanging with trapunto-quilted flowers and curlicues. The face was shaped over a plaster cast. 50 inches high, 40 inches wide, 13 inches deep.
Courtesy, artist

Doll made of stuffed velvet with embroidered mirrors and embellished with crocheted curlicues. By Tony Prescott.

Heavy woven fabric fashioned into an abstract doll shape is embroidered and embellished with crocheted rings, tassels, and beads. By Tony Prescott.

RINGS AND CURLICUES

Novel details made with crochet may be used to embellish crocheted objects, or for adding to other types of needlework for zesty, different, and fun looks. They are fun to create, too. Rings and curlicues are especially easy and effective.

RINGS

Rings may be created in many sizes; all depend on the circle shape to be covered. You can use bone and plastic rings sold in drapery departments; washers, brass curtain hardware, plastic rings cut from six-packs of canned soft drinks, bamboo and wood rings sold in craft shops for macramé and other uses. Of course, the "ring" need not be round; the same procedures can be used with ovals, squares, and amoeboid shapes.

Procedure:

1. Insert the hook through the ring and draw a loop of yarn. Secure the end in place by passing both ends of yarn around the hook; draw through the loop already on the hook. Use this doubled yarn *only* for the first stitch.

2. Continue working single crochet around the ring, keeping the stitches close together so the ring does not show. When the ring is covered, join the first stitch with a slip stitch; cut the yarn and finish off the ends.

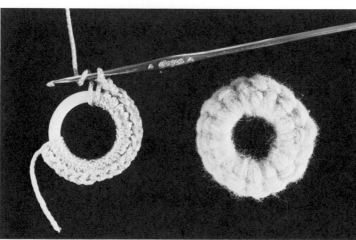

Curlicues

Use your own ingenuity for placing these curlicue cuties. Some ideas may be a "pull" for a zipper end on a purse or sweater. Make several for a cluster at the end of a scarf, the tip of a neckline, the bottom of a pocket. Make them from metallic yarns or mix them up with metallic and regular yarns, shiny and dull finishes, and so forth.

Procedure:

First row: chain 20.

Second row: Work 2 double crochet into the 4th chain. Work 3 double crochet in the next chain and repeat this progression to the end of the chain. Cut the yarn and finish off as shown.

Eskimo soapstone sculptures have the simplified shapes and detailing that can inspire easy-to-make, imaginative, contemporary doll forms.

Linda St. Marie fashioned whimsical dolls from crocheted wool and added bells and beads. Mexican dolls gave her the color ideas she wanted. For the roly-poly shape below, she added a crocheted cotton sunburst medallion with a bead at the bottom.

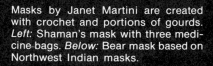

Masks by Janet Martini are created with crochet and portions of gourds. *Left:* Shaman's mask with three medicine bags. *Below:* Bear mask based on Northwest Indian masks.

Sarah Kerr's crocheted mask has negative spaces to emulate designs around the eyes of Indian headwear and totems. The stuffed areas represent warriors' clubs.

Mask with feathered wings by Janet Martini with an African-Oriental derivation.

12. Mix, Mate, Elaborate

NO MATTER WHERE YOU LIVE, FABRICS PRODUCED IN FOREIGN countries have an exotic flavor that whets visual and tactile appetites of those seeking something unusual in the clothing they wear, the objects they make. Not all materials are readily available by the yard, so finding the unique, whether it is a handkerchief-size square or yards of gossamer silk sari cloth, can become an exciting search in itself. After you have an assortment of materials, yarns, threads, beads, and baubles, the question is how to put them together.

Examples throughout the book, and especially those on the following pages, should set smoldering ideas aflame, make itchy fingers busy. Look through your boxes of goodies and think "exotic;" you'll set yourself on a new course of needlework happiness. Take an idea here, a concept there, mix them together, match them up, add a startling trim, and enjoy the smashing results.

Be daring and dramatic in the materials you mix and mate. Try woven fabric from Guatemala with flowered embroidery from the Philippines, a mirrored panel from India, or an ikat woven panel from Peru, then elaborate on your theme with tassels, pompons, buttons, and beads. Try wrapping and braiding, adding ribbons and trims. Give in to your wildest whims. Combine needlework techniques shown in earlier chapters; add a dash of gold thread around a collar and cuff, or beadwork in the design of a mola you buy or make.

Only one word of caution: you can get too carried away with the freedom of folkwear, of garments that use print upon print, color upon color. You can end up with a discordant note rather than a delightful harmony. When you mix and mate, select fabrics with one dominant color and make other colors subordinate in different proportions. If your garment is essentially orange, use lesser amounts of yellow and still smaller amounts of reds or greens.

Diane Powers has an inventive approach to ethnic needlework in her dolls, about 12 to 15 inches high. They are made of a carefully chosen conglomeration of materials gleaned from many cultures.

The final test about your creations is how you feel about them. If you like the way a garment looks and you are comfortable in it, then it is you! It reflects your spirit, your personality. The exotic look is timeless, ageless—a wise and wonderful way to worldliness.

221

Seams, necklines, armholes, hems, and endings of stitched areas often have unusual detailing. These fabrics are machine joined, but the Tacked Herringbone Stitch emulates ethnic joinings. By Elisabeth Schimitschek.

A "capote," or blanket coat, might have inspired Gisela Dennert to use an old army blanket from a resale shop. More inspired is her inventive use of the Randa Stitch for joining the cut edges. Randas are used extensively in Guatemalan and Mexican clothing in many colors and designs. They can run horizontally or vertically.

ETHNIC ELABORATIONS

A study of ethnic clothing reveals embellishments that are as varied and diverse as there are countries that use them. Just as the embroidery stitches themselves become a "needlework" language, some of the less obvious techniques for joining fabrics and making tassels and other embellishments are repeated with minor variations. Once you begin to look for the methods, you'll have an eye-opening experience. For example, in Guatemala weaving looms make fabrics of only a certain width. Therefore, garments requiring longer fabrics are joined with decorative hand stitching because not everyone has access to a sewing machine. The following stitches reappear in many cultures with individualized variations for joining fabrics and for camouflaging the joining. Feel free to improvise any of your own by combining stitches you have learned in earlier chapters.

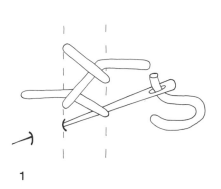

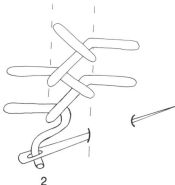

1

2

SEAM JOININGS

1,2 A *Randa Stitch* is an over-and-under stitch used to join two folded-back fabric edges together. The result looks like a Satin Stitch with a ridge down the center; but when made as shown the threads act as knots and prevent the seam from ripping.

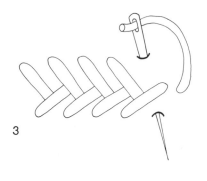

3

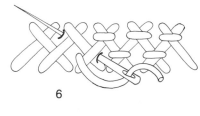

4

3,4 The *Y-Seam Stitch* used for joinery also spans the folded edges of two pieces of cloth butted together.

5 *Fagoting (left)* is a decorative joining for two pieces of cloth allowing a space between.

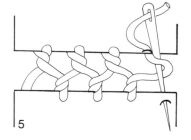

5

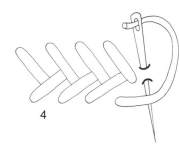

6

6 *Tacked Herringbone Stitch (right)* can be used over a sewn joining for a decorative secondary treatment. The basic Herringbone Stitch (page 15) is accomplished, then a Backstitch is worked over the crossed legs of the stitches.

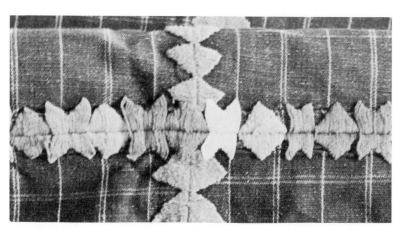

Details of Randa joinings: (*left*) Guatemala, (*above*) Mexico

TASSELS, POMPONS, BEADS, BRAIDS, AND WRAPS

Cultures throughout the world use a delightful variety of different, dangling trims. You'll find them in profusion on the clothing of Afghanistan, Guatemala, Peru, Spain, Africa, American Indians, and so forth. They may be made of yarn, plant fibers, or animal hair, then embellished with shells, tusks, beads, even the backs of clicking beetles that are dry, hollow, and iridescent.

The techniques that follow have been selected from only a few cultures to give you ideas for trim. Then you are on your own. Visit local museums, attend dance and theatre functions presented by different ethnic groups, and study the elements that interest you. If a particular item or technique catches your attention and you don't know how to make it, ask one of the older women in the group. Most likely she will know and be happy to show you how she learned to do it when she was a young girl—or lead you to someone who can help you—with great pleasure.

An embroidered pull from the Orient has beads and a decorative tassel.
Collection, Diane Powers

Barbara Chapman chose a handle from a Persian copper pot and twined a purse mostly of goat hair. The central ornament is an antique beaded rondelle from Afghanistan. The tassels, too, are taken from an Afghani item and added to the purse; they consist of wrapped and knotted lengths of yarn with beads at the tassel tips.

MAKING TASSELS

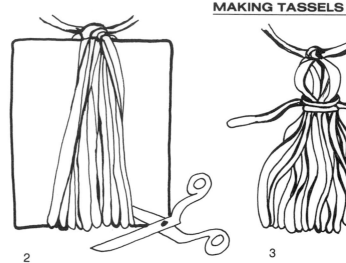

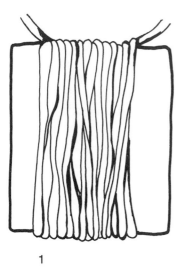

1

2

3

1. Cut a piece of cardboard the length you want the finished tassel to be and a few inches wide. Wrap the yarn vertically around the cardboard until it is the desired thickness.

2. Tie a piece of yarn around the wrapped strands at the top. Cut the strands at the bottom.

3. Remove the cardboard and the basic tassel is ready for any type of decorative treatment. The simplest tassel involves wrapping the yarn horizontally about an inch below the top.

a   b   c   d

Variations of the simple tassel
a. Double top
b. Beads added around the wrapping
c. Beads and colored cloth strips plain or beaded
d. Beads and feathers.

Shaped tassels may be developed for large and small projects. Place a "stuffing" material under the tied yarns, bring the yarns around the object, then wrap, bead, crochet, or stitch. A length of wood dowel is shown here; other objects might be round polyurethane balls or cones. Stuff scrap yarns into plastic food wrap and shape any way you like, then cover with the yarn tassel.

Yarns wrapped around the tassel may be additionally decorated by vertical wraps using needle through all or part of the wrap.

Embroidery and beading around the tassel wrap (*left*). A felt skirt around the tassel, fringed, beaded, and embroidered (*right*).

More tassel ideas (*left*) by Tony Prescott, (*right*) by Mandy Arrington

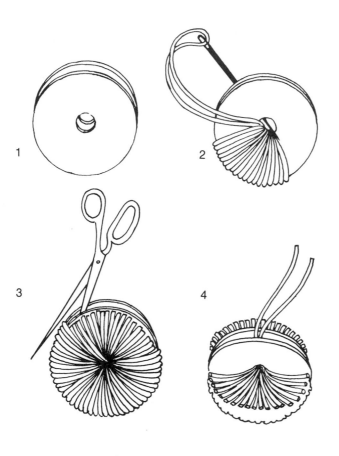

MAKING POMPONS

1. Cut two cardboard doughnuts with a diameter 1½ times the desired size of the pompon (a 3-inch circle equals a 2-inch pompon). The center hole should be large enough to wind all the yarn through. Cut strands of yarns 6 yards long.

2. Thread the tapestry needle and double the thread. Put the cardboard circles together and wrap the circles as shown until the yarn covers the circles and the center hole is filled.

3. Cut between the circles at the outside edge with a sharp scissors.

4. Wind two strands of yarn about 8 inches long between the circles, tie securely. Remove the circles, fluff the yarn into the pompon shape, trim the edges evenly. Attach the pompon with the tie thread.

A Guatemalan woman, off to market, carries garments trimmed with pompons, tassels, and fringes.

A pillow cover from India with embroidered shi sha mirrors has been slit and used for a neck cape with tassels added. By Dona Meilach.

A basic hat can be changed every time
you wear it by taking your cue from the
young lady above. Woven bands with
pompons, and some beads, can be tied
around a hat and layered, or used
individually as the mood moves you. By
Diane Powers.

Coins, beaded lengths, bells, and tassels
decorate a Meo Hill tribe child's hat.

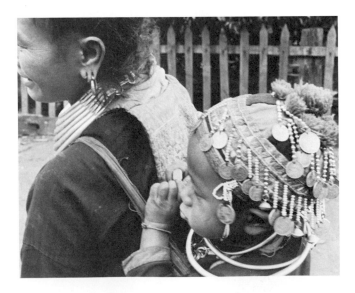

Dorothy Hicks learned how to wrap and couldn't stop until she made a Maypole skirt; a series of wrapped lengths added to a waistband and worn over another garment.

HOW TO WRAP

Wrapping involves winding cords tightly around a core:

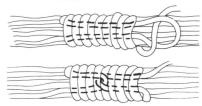

Use one of the lengths in the core and form a loop with one end of the cord and hold the bottom secure. Wrap the cord around all the yarns for the desired length and place the end through the loop. Pull on the loop pulling the end inside. Clip off any loose ends.

When you want to introduce a new color wrapping cord around the core use the following method:

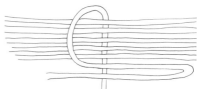

Introduce a new length of cord parallel to the lengths you are wrapping as shown.

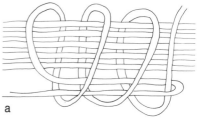

a

Wrap the cord around all the strands and pull the strand (a) which will bring the loop and the loose end under the wraps and secure it. The wrapping should be done very tightly (it is drawn loosely for demonstration).

Gail Louis's application of beads, buttons, ribbons, and whatnot to a backpack bears a striking resemblance to the clothing trim on the Yemenite dress below.

Yemenite dress and detail.
Collection, Stana Coleman,
Evanston, Illinois
Photos, Dee Menagh

Mandy Arrington used the Folkwear pattern for a Turkish coat made of cotton canvas upholstery fabrics. She trimmed it with precious materials with personal meaning, pompons, and velvet. She stenciled, quilted, and embroidered a motif for the center back.

Gayle McGinnis used Turkish medallions, beads, wrapping, and novelty yarns for the tassels of a basket plant hanger.
Collection, Diane Powers

Diane Powers appliquéd a mola onto a fabric shoulder purse and added buttons around it. Across the top of the purse, there is a panel of mirror embroidery from India. Beads and coins are from Afghanistan. The braided tasseled endings are a fun touch.

Barbara Chapman embellished a hand-woven purse with a silk embroidered antique panel from China. The handle and beaded tassels are portions from Afghanistan neckwear.

A purse made with fringes, tassels, beads, buttons, appliqué, and woven panels is today's adaptation of an old carpetbag, functional and decorative. By Diane Powers.

Guatemalan fabric is edged with assorted band weavings in different, but related, designs. A beaded panel with a floppy pompon and beads at the bottom are the decorative front of the purse. By Diane Powers.

←

Diane Powers has incorporated so many objects on this small purse that a description would require an entire page. Study it carefully and see what you can discover.

If you don't want to frame all your needlepoint work, make one into a purse: Diane Powers's butterfly bag is joined at the sides with fabric. Mirrors, beads, tassels, and an embroidered handle are added.

An angel doll by Diane Powers carries a llama from Peru.

A woven basket becomes the base for a cover of assembled ethnic items. By Diane Powers.

A Chinese doll with a silver and beaded headpiece and layer upon layer of fabric with embroidery and appliqué. Decorative dolls are popular in other cultures and become a rich source for deriving your own combinations.

Photographed at
San Diego Museum of Man

Bride doll, front and back views. By Diane Powers.

A peasant doll with appliquéd laces and beads, and hand-stitched facial features. By Twyla Cottrell.

Elisabeth Schimitschek combines a mola with Guatemalan woven fabric. She simulates ethnic joinery with a Tacked Herringbone Stitch and plain Herringbone Stitches.

Above, right:
Assembled and appliquéd embroidered panels from Turkey are mated with ribbons of a similar feeling and added to the front and back of a long tunic. By Tony Prescott.

Barbara Chapman made a red tunic of Guatemalan fabric, and appliquéd a mola on the center front. The cuffs are pieces of Afghanistan petit point with fringe from a meditation scarf from Uzbek, Russia.

Opposite page:
Combined fabrics and motifs also make an unusual wall hanging. Lucy Anderson used a panel from India and padded the elephant portion from the back in a trapunto technique. She appliqued ribbons, candle shapes, and the awning-type top and elaborated them with stitchery, mirrors, tassels, and beads.

Buttons, ribbons, and a printed panel from a tablecloth from India are added to a peasant-style cotton dress. By Janet Martini.

A long white dress has been trimmed with woven fabrics from Guatemala. By Edmee Forshey.

Three generations. Guatemala.
Photo study, Mel Meilach

13. Patterns—Eclectic Ethnic

GARMENTS WORN BY PEOPLES THROUGHOUT THE WORLD, whether they are called peasant, ethnic, or folkwear, are tremendously varied. Within one culture, however, the garment styles remain relatively constant through the years, with changes occurring gradually over long periods of time. And within that culture the styles are ageless, timeless, always functional.

We often think that some of the indigenous garments we see worn by peoples of various cultures in today's magazines are affectations for the camera, for special holidays, for outstanding events. While some peoples have adopted Western dress, an astonishing number of cultures retain their inherent clothing style because it suits their needs. It is heartwarming, for example, to travel in the back areas of Guatemala and discover that the richly embroidered blouses, the intricately woven skirts of hand-dyed fabrics in dizzying patterns are everyday dress. In Afghanistan, in Tunisia, Thailand, Indonesia, and other countries we have visited, people retain the styles of their ancestors.

Ironically these "ageless styles," which have become high style for the European and American designer, can become ageless in our own wardrobes. The handmade item can be perennially fresh and appealing— an antidote for the planned obsolescence that exists in many purchases we make today.

Clothing for countless cultures throughout the ages has been dictated by several factors: the ability of hands to shape the cloth it has available, the terrain, the need for movement, the climate, and social status.

Man's first clothes were made from skins of animals. The size of the skin and the ability to piece sections together dictated the cut of the garment.

When weaving was introduced, the width of cloth made on available looms necessitated certain patterns that resulted in as little waste as possible. Earliest loom-woven pieces were not even sewn; rather, the woven lengths were wrapped about the body. The poncho was probably one of the earliest sewn garments; the woven panels were stitched together and a slit or hole made for the head.

Othello Coat. Frances Bardacke. Black and white linen with fringe, rickrack, and crocheted doily trim (see page 252 for front view and pattern).

241

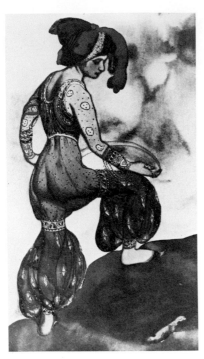

The costume of the Blue Sultan by designer Leon Bakst from "Scheherazade" combines shaping and design inspired by the Middle Eastern culture.

The second sewn garment is believed to have been the shirt style, which had many names in certain periods and different areas, for example, the shift, robe, tunic, smock, dress, frock, chemise, and so on. It could be woven on a wide loom to create different lengths. Sometimes the sleeve width was extended during the weaving process. Eventually, the shirt with fullness around the neck developed, and a collar was added.

A study of garments and costumes around the world in various historical periods can keep you so absorbed you may never have time to sew or to embellish the garments you want to make. To save you time, we offer a selection of patterns that have been adapted to contemporary needs and styles. On the body, they may look complex, but an analysis of the pattern reveals that they are incredibly simple—most of the pieces are geometric shapes with seams that are easily mated. They can be embellished with any of the ideas offered throughout the book.

BEFORE YOU BEGIN

The following patterns are taken directly from ethnic garments or are purposely adapted to current tastes. The measurements given are suited to approximately size 10-12. They are usually full and do not conform to tight body contours, so they can be readily adjusted to become larger or smaller by adding or subtracting a few inches. Arm and shoulder widths and lengths are the main consideration.

In all the patterns you will observe that the parts are usually rectangles or squares, so placing the pattern on fabric and cutting are simple. Fitting problems should be minimal because the garments usually have straight seams and require little cutting into the fabric and little fabric waste. Always save cut-out scraps for appliqué onto the garment later or for additions to other garments.

The essential idea for use of the pattern is to feel free to mix anything you like. The possibilities are unlimited; the same pattern offered for a shirt can be lengthened to become a knee-length or full-length dress. The Kendo jacket (page 256, for example) may be used for a short "hippari," a hip-length garment, or lengthened for a kimono. The same styles may be used for large and small figures, for adults or children. Many of the garments can be adapted for men or women. One basic pattern created in different fabrics and embellished individually can result in a wardrobe of infinite variety.

CUTTING

Mark your patterns on the wrong side of the fabric. If necessary, make a paper or scrap fabric pattern first to determine fit and the size of neck openings. Small circles can be marked with a dish or compass. For a large circle tie a length of string around a pencil. Hold the string end at the fabric center and swing the pencil around. Place the pattern edges along the straight weave of the fabric.

NOTE: ALL PATTERNS REQUIRE AN ADDITION FOR SEAM ALLOWANCE OF YOUR PREFERENCE.

SEWING

In many cultures sewing machines do not exist and before they were invented all seams were joined by hand. Sewing the straight seams can easily be accomplished by hand or machine by the neophyte or the experienced seamstress. This is not basically a how-to-sew book, so if you are unfamiliar with neck facings and seam placements, refer to a sewing book or use available patterns with sewing directions from Folkwear, Butterick, Vogue, Simplicity, and so forth. With a little experience one can easily "read" the patterns and know how to assemble the parts. No matter how you finish a piece you really can't go too far wrong. If it doesn't fit or if a seam doesn't look quite right, you can always revise and embellish the area with embroidery, appliqué, or other addition.

FABRICS

The range of fabric choices is extensive. Cottons, linens, synthetics, wools, and so forth, available from fabric shops, are perfect. Plan to use unconventional materials such as drapery and upholstery fabrics, bedspreads, tablecloths, and materials pieced together from other clothing and from other objects. Select fabrics not only for their weight and color, but also for an interesting texture, or weave, that can be embellished as your designer's eye imagines.

The charts below and on the following pages are offered for your convenience.

Egyptian shirt from a Folkwear pattern is a basic caftan cut with rectangular front and back panel, rectangle side panels, and sleeves. Most ethnic garments can readily be folded flat.

Courtesy, Folkwear

YOUR MEASUREMENTS

Use the chart below to record your measurements; make a similar chart for everyone for whom you plan to make a garment.

Shoulder width_____

Length from shoulder to elbow_____

Length from underarm to wrist _____

Bust—around widest part_____

Hips—around widest part_____

Length from shoulder to center of bust _____

Length from underarm to waist_____

Neck circumference _____

Length from shoulder to waist _____

Length from shoulder to hip _____

Length from shoulder to knee_____

Length from shoulder to hemline above shoes or to floor

(for long garments) _____

Around upper arm_____Around wrist_____

Length from waist to hem (for short dress)_____

Length from waist to floor (for long dress) _____

Crotch to cuff (for pants)_____

METRIC EQUIVALENCY CHART

CONVERTING INCHES TO CENTIMETERS AND YARDS TO METERS

This chart provides standard equivalents as approved by the Pattern Fashion Industry.

mm—millimeters   cm—centimeters   m—meters

INCHES INTO MILLIMETERS AND CENTIMETERS
(Slightly rounded for your convenience)

inches	mm		cm	inches	cm	inches	cm
⅛	3mm			7	18	29	73,5
¼	6mm			8	20,5	30	76
⅜	10mm	or	1cm	9	23	31	79
½	13mm	or	1,3cm	10	25,5	32	81,5
⅝	15mm	or	1,5cm	11	28	33	84
¾	20mm	or	2cm	12	30,5	34	86,5
⅞	22mm	or	2,2cm	13	33	35	89
1	25mm	or	2.5cm	14	35.5	36	91,5
1¼	32mm	or	3,2cm	15	38	37	94
1½	38mm	or	3.8cm	16	40,5	38	96.5
1¾	45mm	or	4,5cm	17	43	39	99
2	50mm	or	5cm	18	46	40	101,5
2½	65mm	or	6,5cm	19	48,5	41	104
3	75mm	or	7,5cm	20	51	42	106,5
3½	90mm	or	9cm	21	53,5	43	109
4	100mm	or	10cm	22	56	44	112
4½	115mm	or	11,5cm	23	58,5	45	114,5
5	125mm	or	12,5cm	24	61	46	117
5½	140mm	or	14cm	25	63,5	47	119,5
6	150mm	or	15cm	26	66	48	122
				27	68,5	49	124,5
				28	71	50	127

YARDS TO METERS
(Slightly rounded for your convenience)

yards	meters	yards	meters	yards	meters	yards	meters	yards	meters
⅛	0,15	2⅛	1,95	4⅛	3,80	6⅛	5,60	8⅛	7,45
¼	0,25	2¼	2,10	4¼	3,90	6¼	5,75	8¼	7,55
⅜	0,35	2⅜	2,20	4⅜	4,00	6⅜	5,85	8⅜	7,70
½	0,50	2½	2,30	4½	4,15	6½	5,95	8½	7,80
⅝	0,60	2⅝	2,40	4⅝	4,25	6⅝	6,10	8⅝	7,90
¾	0,70	2¾	2,55	4¾	4,35	6¾	6,20	8¾	8,00
⅞	0,80	2⅞	2,65	4⅞	4,50	6⅞	6,30	8⅞	8,15
1	0,95	3	2,75	5	4,60	7	6,40	9	8,25
1⅛	1,05	3⅛	2,90	5⅛	4,70	7⅛	6,55	9⅛	8,35
1¼	1,15	3¼	3,00	5¼	4,80	7¼	6,65	9¼	8,50
1⅜	1,30	3⅜	3,10	5⅜	4,95	7⅜	6,75	9⅜	8,60
1½	1,40	3½	3,20	5½	5,05	7½	6,90	9½	8,70
1⅝	1,50	3⅝	3,35	5⅝	5,15	7⅝	7,00	9⅝	8,80
1¾	1,60	3¾	3,45	5¾	5,30	7¾	7,10	9¾	8,95
1⅞	1,75	3⅞	3,55	5⅞	5,40	7⅞	7,20	9⅞	9,05
2	1,85	4	3,70	6	5,50	8	7,35	10	9,15

TO DETERMINE SIZE

Always take body measurements and adjust the given dimensions of the patterns as required. Always measure over undergarments and allow ample room for fullness. Check washing/cleaning directions of the fabrics you plan to use and allow for shrinkage where necessary.

AVERAGE BODY MEASUREMENTS

MISSES

Size	6	8	10	12	14	16	18	
Bust	30½	31½	32½	34	36	38	40	ins.
Waist	22	23	24	25½	27	29	31	''
Hip	32½	33½	34½	36	38	40	42	''

WOMEN

Size	38	40	42	44	46	48	
Bust	42	44	46	48	50	52	ins.
Waist	34	36	38	40½	43	45½	''
Hip	44	46	48	50	52	54	''

MEN

Size	34	36	38	40	42	44	
Chest	34	36	38	40	42	44	ins.
Waist	30	32	34	36	38	40	''

YOUNG JUNIORS/TEENS

Size	7/8	9/10	11/12	13/14	
Bust	29	30½	32	33½	ins.
Waist	23	24	25	26	''
Hip	32	33½	35	36½	''

JUNIORS

Size	7	9	11	13	15	
Bust	31	32	33½	35	37	ins.
Waist	22½	23½	24½	26	28	''
Hip	33	34	35½	37	39	''

INFANTS AND GIRLS

Size	6 mos.	1	2	3	4	6	8	10	12	14	
Chest	19	20	21	22	23	24	27	28½	30	32	ins.
Waist	19	19½	20	20½	21	22	23½	24½	25½	26½	''
Hip	20	21	22	23	24	26	28	30	32	34	''
Height	22	25	29	31	33	37	41	45	49	53	''

BOYS

Size	1	2	3	4	6	8	10	12	14	16	
Chest	20	21	22	23	24	26	28	30	32	34	ins.
Waist	19½	20	20½	21	22	23	24	25½	27	29	''
Neck					11	11½	12	12½	13½	14	''
Hip	20	21	22	23	25	27	29	31	33	35½	''
Height	25	29	31	33	37	41	45	49	53	55	''

FESTIVE VEST

A vest design adapted from the Slavic countries in hand-weave with surface embroidery by Bucky King makes a marvelous pattern for an incredible variety of treatments and uses. In Poland, Hungary, Yugoslavia, needlework of individualistic and symbolic patterning was developed over the entire garment or only around the borders.

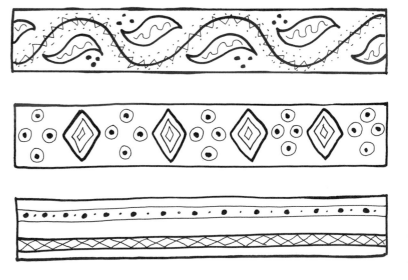

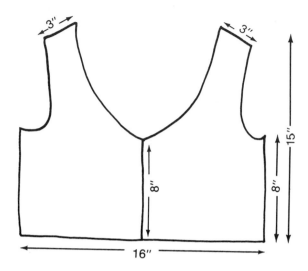

The vest front is flat with no shaping and cut from a rectangle of fabric. Adjust the bust size as necessary; darts could be worked in under the bust line if desired, and depending upon the material used.

The two front panels can be made so they do not close and have decorative closures such as lacing, ties, loops, and buttons, and Chinese or Oriental frogs. Or they may be cut so the fronts overlap, with buttons and buttonholes or snaps.

For decorative trim, use embroidery, embroidery with appliqué, ribbons, buttons, or combinations of all techniques.

Fabric suggestions are cotton, linen, wool, synthetics, or heavy upholstery materials. If the vest is made of felt you can eliminate binding or turning under the edges. The vest may be lined.

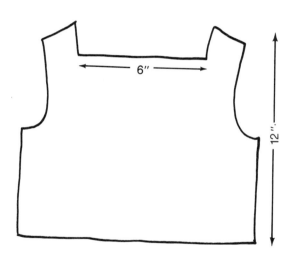

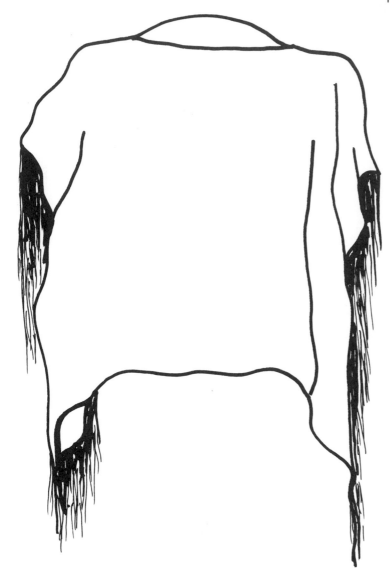

THE CLASSIC HUIPIL

The huipil, a basic garment in the wardrobe of the Mexican, can be equally versatile and infinitely varied for many occasions in anyone's wardrobe. The huipil, also called a poncho, in its simplest form is a piece of cloth with a hole in the center for the head. It probably dates from pre-Hispanic times. It became a "sewn" garment when the fabric was folded in half and sewn down the sides to close it and become a sleeveless shirt.

The huipil was worn by both men and women but with a minor differentiation. The men's huipil was made as described above. A woven striped material was used, which folded so the stripes were worn vertically on the body. The women's garment had the stripes and the seam running horizontally around the body.

The huipil is made by joining two lengths of cloth and leaving a slit for the head. It may be quickly assembled from two prehemmed scarves about 45 inches long and 12 inches wide with a 16-inch opening for the neckline.

Wear the huipil with the fold at the shoulders, add fringe or other decoration and ties at the sides, or close the side seams to the armhole. The rectangles can be larger and worn so the ends pull over the wrist as in Susan Nelson's handwoven huipil (*left*). The decoration was inspired by the American Indians and decorated with bands of thin metal and buttons. Similar effects could be achieved with ribbon appliqué or direct embroidery.

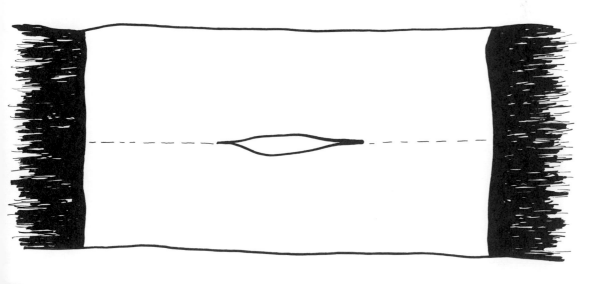

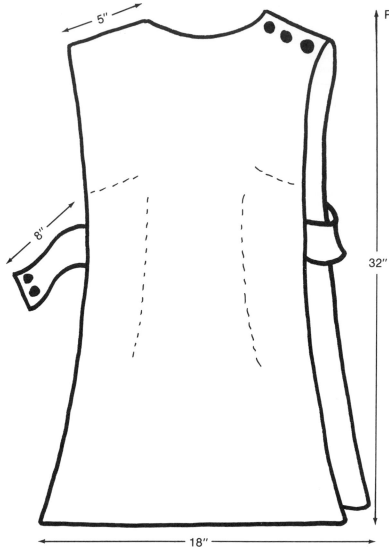

THE TERRIFIC TABARD

Historically, the tabard was a tunic worn by a knight over his armor and emblazoned with his coat of arms. Later the heralds also wore it, for displaying the heraldic symbols. In France, about the middle of the fifteenth century, it became a part of the male attire and eventually was brought into England. The tabard, a sleeveless garment, may be wholly or partially open at the sides.

The tabard shown is completely made of Guatemalan fabric and lined with rayon. The basic front and back is a rectangle with a rounded neckline and the shoulders cut at a slight angle. A closure on one shoulder may be buttoned or secured with a Velcro closure. The belt bands that hold the front and back together can have two sets of hooks or snaps for adjustability. The classic tabard is about hip length, but it can be varied for the most flattering length desired—just below the waist or above the knees.

The tabard shown is also slightly fitted in the front with two sets of darts, one at the bust line and one to nip in the waistline. The darts are optional.

This basic design may be varied: change the neckline to a front slit opening and sew both shoulders completely so it may be slipped over the head, making the front neckline deeper. Or change the neckline to a square front, and so forth. It may be embellished with a delightful array of embroidery or appliqué to recall the original use—to display a family coat of arms, or a decorative monogram.

OTHELLO COAT

Frances Bardacke observed a costume made for an actor in the Shakespearean drama *Othello* and re-created the design in an ethnic idiom (see photograph page 240). She used boldly patterned black and white linen from a tablecloth with a self-patterned border of large and small rectangles. All pieces are assembled with decorative machine embroidery over the joinings. Appliquéd lace doilies repeat the diamond in the pattern for an additional trim on the solid black insert in the back center shoulder.

Like most ethnic garments illustrated, the entire coat folds flat, yet it drapes beautifully because of the design. The front angles up at the hem because the sleeves become off-centered in the arrangement. In the pattern the sleeves appear to face in the wrong direction, but when the garment is worn, it all falls into place in a marvelous arrangement of flowing folds.

Make the Othello coat in linen for a dramatic hostess coat, in silk or satin for an evening wrap, in wool for cooler weather, and even in terry toweling for a beach robe. It is the ultimate in versatility and it feels magnificent when it is worn. Our thanks to Frances Bardacke for sharing this garment design with us.

1. The back may be one solid rectangle, or pieced to extend fabric and create design elements. When stitching front and back together at top, leave opening for armholes and trim with fringe.

2. Point X actually becomes the center back of the neckline, and the three panels shown across the front fall across the back shoulders. Seam YY becomes the shoulder line. However, front and back, designated as shown in the pattern, are cut the same length.

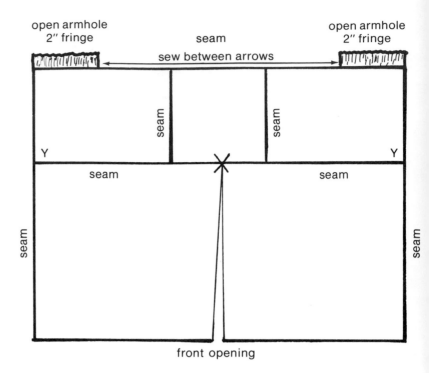

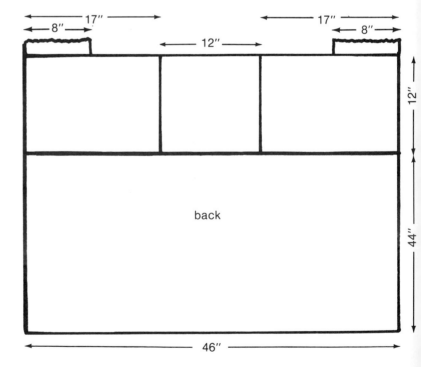

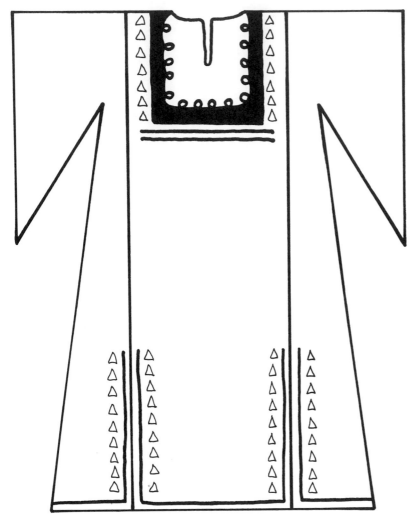

ECLECTIC DRESS

A Middle Eastern shirt dress is normally made of a rectangle of fabric for the front and back with side panels and sleeves that are also rectangular (see Egyptian shirt, Folkwear pattern (page 243). Here it has been varied with an Oriental sleeve added and the side panels flared. This illustrates the ease with which ethnic patterns can be altered to become eclectic. They are in the spirit of today, when we feel free to mix anything we like.

And in the spirit of mixing, think of varying the dress by making the front panel a print and the side panels solid, for example. Or reverse and repeat the print of the side panels as the trim around the neck and hem.

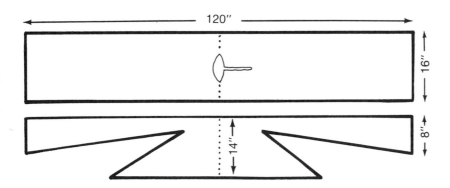

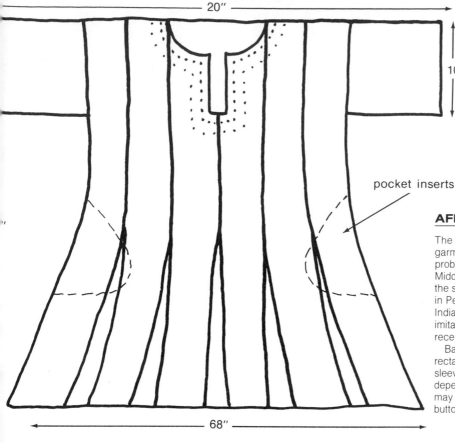

20"

10"

pocket inserts

68"

AFRI-CAFTAN

The basic caftan, a long or short full garment with a flowing appearance, probably originated in the Oriental and Middle Eastern countries. Variations of the simply styled garment have appeared in Persia, Arabia, China, and among East Indian groups. It has enjoyed many imitations throughout the years, and recently in American fashions.

Basically the caftan is composed of a rectangular front and back panel. The sleeves may be square or rectangular, depending upon the length desired. It may be made to slip over the head or button down the front.

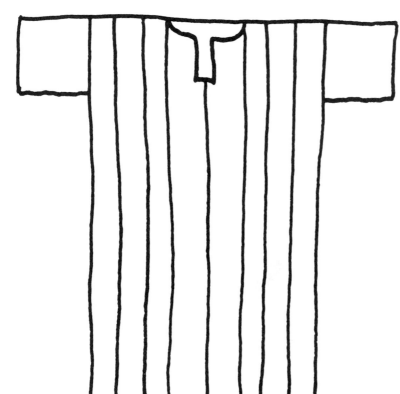

The Africans have a variation of the caftan that is super for contemporary ethnic designs because it permits you to use a wide variety of prints. The African garment probably originated because of the narrow widths of fabric woven on looms in some of the countries, particularly Nigeria, which is known for its kenté cloth—4-inch bands of woven fabric.

In this version the 4-inch strips are sewn together to form the cloth; then an additional 2-inch strip of fabric in another pattern is inserted as a gusset between each strip. Observe that each is set in at a slightly different height above waist level to give the garment additional flair.

A neck facing (made from old flour bags in the original) is used; two pockets are inserted between the side seams. Machine or hand embroidery may be added around the neckline.

This basic pattern can be embellished with embroidery, or make it from several different fabric panels and wear with a smashing piece of ethnic jewelry.

Depending on the fabric available:
1. The front and back can be treated as one piece of material and made of a rectangle to measure from front hem to back hem with a hole cut for the neck. Sleeve shapes are added in.
2. Or cut one front and one back and sew together at the shoulder. Then add side panels or sleeves as necessary.

KENDO COAT

The basic Oriental kimono has many variations and names. Illustrated is a "kendo" coat adapted for everyday wear. The kendo coat is, in reality, a padded jacket worn by Japanese fencers to protect them from the blade point. In this version, the jacket is completely reversible; the Running Stitch pattern (called a Kogin Stitch in Japanese) changes from small to large diamonds separated by a horizontal stitch line around the body for design, not structure. The garment is cut of rectangles, there are no seams at the shoulders, and the rectangular sleeve pattern is set in so that when it is worn it drops below the shoulder arm line. The kendo has a slit in the center back to allow greater freedom in movement for the fencer, unlike the kimono, or aboriginal coat, shown on the following page.

A hippari coat is made exactly like the kendo coat but is shorter and falls just above the hipline.

Collection, Dona Meilach

The sleeve pattern may be varied as shown.

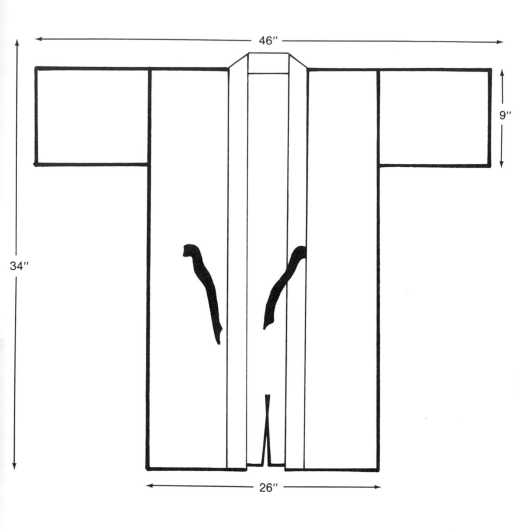

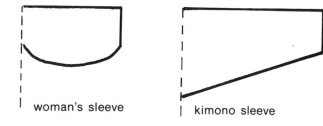

woman's sleeve   kimono sleeve

Aboriginal coat, nineteenth-century. Cotton appliqué.
Collection, Mr. & Mrs. Jerry Martin
Courtesy, Mingei-Folk Arts of Japan

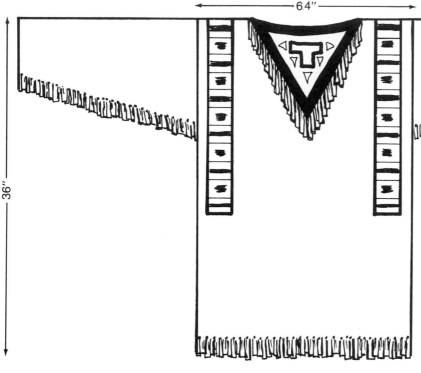

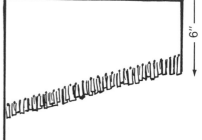

AMERICAN INDIAN CEREMONIAL SHIRT

It is sometimes startling to observe how close in pattern the garments of peoples are in different countries at different times. Man's need to clothe himself using simple cut and construction of the available fabric is evident in this American Indian ceremonial shirt originally made in leather. Compare it with the cotton appliqué Oriental kimono-style coat at left.

The American Indian shirt fits more closely to the body than the kimono and is a slipover rather than a front wrap. But the rectangular front-and-back panel and set-in sleeves are the same.

The shirt may be made of any modern fabric as well as suede or leather. The designs may be painted on or stitched and appliquéd in any of the Indian patterns shown here and elsewhere in the book. You may also paint the fringe area rather than sew on real fringe. Always paint or color the fringe band first, then cut it. Use fabric paints, waterproof colored marker, or silk screen for a basic design that may be emphasized with stitchery.

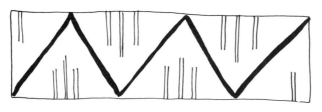

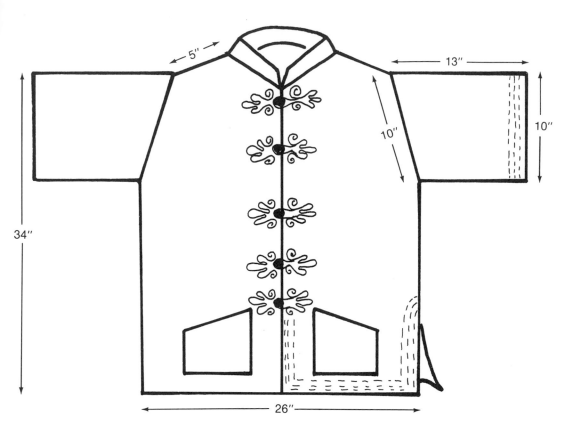

THAI SHIRT

Thai men wear clothes that are similar in design to the garments of their Oriental neighbors. A cotton shirt with slits at the side can be readily embroidered and worn by men or boys. It is so basic that it can be adapted to a woman's or girl's shirt, too. The front and back are cut rectangles with the shoulders shaped and sleeves set into angled armholes. The closures shown are the Oriental frogs made of covered cord, but anything can be used.

Make the shirt of cotton or permanent-press fabric, linen, or any desired material. A longer version can become a shirt dress.

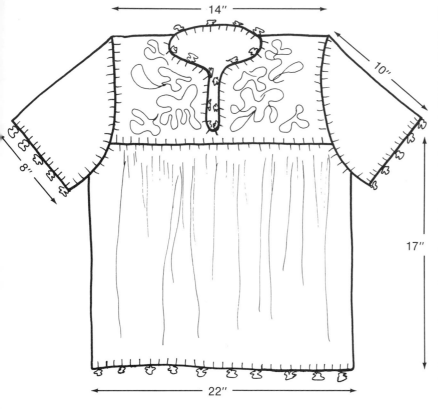

PHILIPPINE BLOUSE

A cotton overblouse completely hand-made and the parts joined with crocheted Chain Stitching is a replica of the type worn by royalty in the Islands during the sixteenth-century. Today's blouse has all fabric shapes joined by closed and open handwork in linen thread. An additional detail is the punch needlework in a floral pattern on the yoke (see detail page 69).

The beauty of this garment is that it may be made by anyone who does not own a sewing machine. The same crochet Chain Stitch used to join the panels is worked around the neckline, bottom edge, and sleeves; it is combined with a Clover-leaf Stitch every 14th chain. The belt is optional.

The overblouse is made of light blue cotton, but it can be effective in dressier materials and bright colors. Individual panels may be varied in prints and solids for another unique look.

Use the Igolochkoy needle for the punchwork texture in any pattern you like. Or substitute the punch needlework with surface embroidery if you prefer.

The back and front are the same size panels with the exception of the neckline. The yoke, with the punch needlework, is faced so the looping will not pull out.

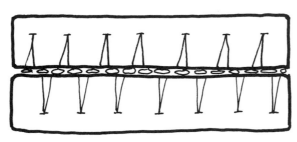

Crochet Chain Stitch

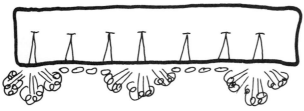

Clover-leaf

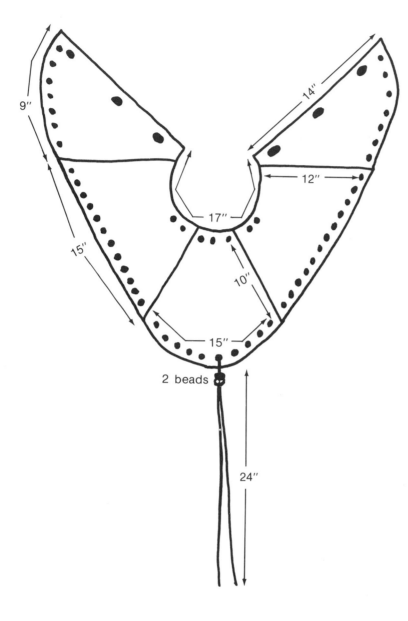

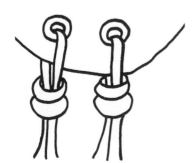

2 beads

WOODLAND CAPE-COLLAR

Ethnic inspiration for a high-style cape or collar makes for an ageless accessory. It is a takeoff of the costume worn by the girls of the American Woodland Indians. With the long Indian-style beaded suede fringe, the cape is frivolous, swinging, attractive, and dramatic. Every dangling fringe vibrates with the body movement.

Without the fringe, the cape can be used as a wide collar; the cut and piecing-together of the parts make it lie flat and perfectly contoured. You may wish to alter the depth of the front and back depending upon your size and the garment it is to accessorize. Use snaps for the back closure.

The cape works beautifully in heavy suede, but it can also be made of bulky fabric with a lining or of the new suede cloths. The depth of the cut cries out for the needleworker to use it for beading, embroidery, shadow appliqué, and reverse appliqué. Try it, too, in woven fabrics from other countries, and then add shi sha mirrors or dangling beading for fringe.

The holes around the edge and the collar front may be made with grommets used in leatherwork or embroidered with a Buttonhole Stitch by hand or machine depending upon the fringe treatment to be used. Ready-made fringe could be attached to the underside of the hem for another effect.

This pattern is so versatile that we wouldn't be surprised if other cultures "took" it from us—and the entire route of eclecticism would come full circle.

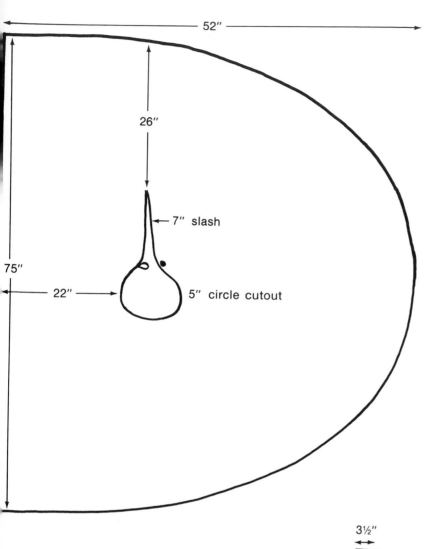

52"

26"

← 7" slash

75"

22" →

5" circle cutout

3½"

9½"

60"

76"

INSPIRATION—INDIA

The half of a circle cape with an off-centered neckline seemed so blatantly a takeoff of ethnic capes that we could not resist offering it here. It is a commercial design that you can easily emulate and embellish. Worn with an off-the-shoulder or one-shoulder garment, the effect is stunning. It can be worn also with any classic dress or pant outfit.

The elemental simplicity of the garment points up the basic premise of ethnic needlework: often the simpler the cut, the greater the result in terms of fabric usage and wearability that is ageless, and always in good taste. The dress, in cotton jersey, is basically made of two rectangles tapered at the waist with the necessary cuts for the armholes and neckline. Both are faced with a piece of fabric and interfacing to prevent the material from stretching.

The nylon chiffon cape, in matching print, hangs loosely and flowingly. It can be made of heavier woven fabric and of shimmering silks and satins, depending upon the need. It may be edged with trim or embroidery. Anyway you visualize and develop it, it has to be one of the most complimented outfits in your wardrobe.

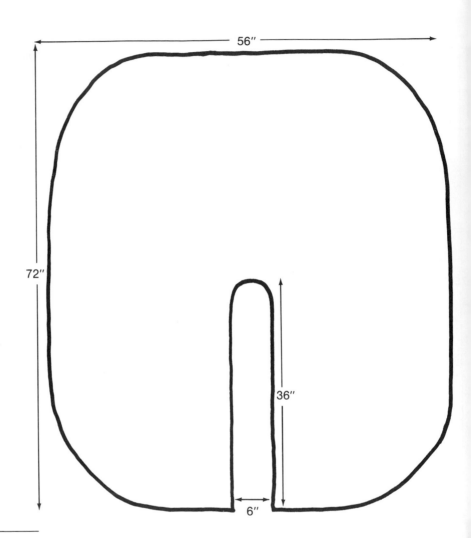

CAPE, UPDATE

The inspiration for this spectacular, versatile, and luxurious cape is believed to be South American, though capes have been used by man for centuries in almost every culture. By making the cape oval rather than circular the elongated ends can be draped about the body in myriad ways.

This cape update is made from double-knit wool. The outer edge is stitched with a machine zigzag that results in a slightly rippled edge, so that either side is the "right" side. A folded-back hem is not advised as it would create a right and wrong side, which would be less attractive as the garment is wrapped about the body.

The edge may also be crocheted, fringed, or ribbon-bound. The large expanse of fabric is a natural "canvas" for any of the exotic needlework techniques and designs illustrated throughout the book.

Selected Bibliography

This bibliography is arranged in three categories. These are "selected" as being among the most helpful that we have found. It does not preclude the hundreds of other available volumes on the subjects; some may be more specific for your interests, and you are encouraged to search them out through your library. Consult *Subject Guide to Books in Print* (for current books) and *The Cumulative Book Index.* Also consult museum booklets found in specific library indexes, magazines from various cultures, and photograph files. To locate the addresses of publishers, consult *The American Book Trade Directory.*

I. NEEDLEWORK TECHNIQUES AND CLOTHING PATTERNS

Bath, Virginia Churchill. *Embroidery Masterworks.* Chicago: Henry Regnery Co., 1972.

Burnham, Dorothy K. *Cut My Cote.* Toronto, Ontario, Canada: Royal Ontario Museum, 1973.

Caulfeild, Sophia, and Saward, Blanche. *The Dictionary of Needlework.* New York: Arno Press, 1972. (Facsimile of 1882 edition.)

Clabburn, Pamela. *The Needleworker's Dictionary.* New York: Wm. Morrow & Co., Inc., 1976.

Coats, J. & P. *100 Embroidery Stitches.* Glasgow: Coats Sewing Group, 1967.

Cordello, Becky Stevens, ed. *Needlework Classics.* New York: Butterick Publishing, 1976.

Dawson, Barbara. *Metal Thread Embroidery.* New York: Taplinger Publishing Co., 1969.

de Dillmont, Thérèse. *Encyclopedia of Needlework.* Mulhouse, France: D.M.C. Library, n.d.

Emery, Irene. *The Primary Structures of Fabrics.* Washington, D.C.: The Textile Museum, 1966.

Enthoven, Jacqueline. *The Stitches of Creative Embroidery.* New York: Van Nostrand Reinhold Co., 1964.

———*Stitches with Variations.* San Ramon, California: Sunset Designs, 1976.

Ewers, John C. *Blackfeet Crafts.* Washington, D.C.: Bureau of Indian Affairs, U.S. Department of Interior, 1945.

Fanning, Robbie. *Decorative Machine Stitchery.* New York: Butterick, 1976.

The Golden Hands Complete Book of Embroidery (ed.). New York: Random House, 1973.

Goodman, Frances Schaill. *The Embroidery of Mexico and Guatemala.* New York: Charles Scribner's Sons, 1976.

Gostelow, Mary. *A World of Embroidery.* New York: Charles Scribner's Sons, 1975.

Holderness, Esther R. *Peasant Chic.* New York: Hawthorn Books, Inc., 1977.

Hunt, W. Ben. *Indian Crafts and Lore.* New York: Golden Press, 1976.

Karasz, Mariska. *Adventures in Stitches.* New York: Funk & Wagnalls, Inc., 1959.

Lane, Rose Wilder. *Woman's Day Book of American Needlework.* New York: Simon and Schuster, 1963.

Lewis, Alfred Allan. *Mountain Artisans Quilting Book.* New York: Macmillan Publishing Co., Inc., 1973.

Lillow, Ira. *Designs for Machine Embroidery.* Newton Centre, Massachusetts: Charles T. Branford Co., 1975.

Lyford, Carrie A. *Quill and Beadwork of the Western Sioux.* Washington, D.C.: Bureau of Indian Affairs, U.S. Department of Interior, 1940.

Marein, Shirley. *Stitchery, Needlepoint, Appliqué and Patchwork.* New York: Viking Press, 1974.

McCall's (ed.). *How to Quilt It.* Books I and II. New York: The McCall Pattern Co., 1973.

McKain, Sharon. *The Great Noank Quilt Factory.* New York: Random House/Pequot Press, 1974.

Meilach, Dona Z. *Creating Art from Fibers and Fabrics.* Chicago: Henry Regnery Co., 1972.

Meilach, Dona Z., and Snow, Lee Erlin. Creative Stitchery. Chicago: Henry Regnery Co., 1969.

Murphy, Marjorie. *Beadwork of American Indian Designs.* New York: Watson-Guptill Publications, 1974.

Orchard, William C. *Beads and Beadwork of the American Indians.* New York: Museum of the American Indian, Heye Foundation, 1929.

——*The Technique of Porcupine-quill Decoration Among the North American Indians.* New York: Museum of the American Indian, Heye Foundation, 1916.

A Portfolio of Folk Costume Patterns. vols. 1 & 2. Santa Fe, New Mexico: Museum of International Folk Art, 1971.

Puckett, Marjorie, and Giberson, Gail. *Primarily Patchwork.* Redlands, California: Cabincraft, 1975.

Shears, Evangeline, and Fielding, Diantha. *Appliqué.* New York: Watson-Guptill Publications, 1972.

Stribling, Mary Lou. *Crafts from North American Indian Arts.* New York: Crown Publishers, Inc., 1975.

Sunset (ed.), *Clothing Decoration.* Menlo Park, California: Lane Publishing Co., 1977.

——*Quilting and Patchwork.* Menlo Park, California: Lane Publishing Co., 1973.

Ramazanŏglu, Gülseren. *Turkish Embroidery.* New York: Van Nostrand Reinhold Co., 1976.

Wildschut, William, and Ewers, John C. *Crow Indian Beadwork.* New York: Heye Foundation, Museum of the American Indian, 1959.

Wilson, Erica. *Erica Wilson's Embroidery Book.* New York: Charles Scribner's Sons, 1973.

II. INSPIRATION FOR DESIGNS

Attenborough, David. *The Tribal Eye*. New York: W. W. Norton & Co., 1977.

The Cashinahua of Eastern Peru. Bristol, Rhode Island: The Haffenreffer Museum of Anthropology, 1975.

Christie, Archibald H. *Pattern Design*. New York: Dover, 1969 (reprint of 1910 *Traditional Methods of Pattern Designing*).

Denver Art Museum, Department of Indian Art, Denver, Colorado. "Parfleches and Other Rawhide Articles," Leaflet No. 77–78. "Plains Beads and Beadwork Designs," Leaflet No. 73–74. "Porcupine Quillwork," Leaflet No. 103.

Enciso, Jorge. *Design Motifs of Ancient Mexico*. New York: Dover, 1947.

Fagg, William (ed.). *The Living Arts of Nigeria*. New York: Macmillan Publishing Co., Inc., 1971.

Fewkes, Jesse Walter. *Designs on Prehistoric Hopi Pottery*. New York: Dover, 1973 reprint of 1911 edition.

Glubock, Shirley. *The Art of the Woodland Indians*. New York: Macmillan Publishing Co., Inc., 1976.

Harris, J. R. *Egyptian Art*. London: Spring Books, Paul Hamlyn, 1966.

Howard, Constance. *Inspiration for Embroidery*. 2nd ed. London: B. T. Batsford, 1967.

Kennedy, Paul E. *North American Indian Design Coloring Book*. New York: Dover, 1971.

Lichten, Frances. *Folk Art Motifs of Pennsylvania*. New York: Dover, 1976.

Loeb, Marcia. *Pennsylvania Dutch Needlepoint Designs*. New York: Dover, 1976.

Lothrop, Samuel Kirkland. *Pre-Columbian Designs from Panama. (Coclé Pottery)*. New York: Dover, 1976.

Meilach, Dona Z. *The Artist's Eye*. Chicago: Henry Regnery Co., 1972.

Meilach, Dona Z., and Hinz, Bill and Jay. *How to Create Your Own Designs*. New York: Doubleday, 1975.

Menten, Theodore (ed.). *Japanese Border Designs*. New York: Dover, 1975.

Newman, Thelma R. *Contemporary African Arts and Crafts*. New York: Crown Publishers, Inc., 1974.

——*Contemporary Southeast Asian Arts and Crafts,* New York: Crown Publishers, Inc., 1977.

Nuttall, Zelia (ed.). *The Codex Nuttall*. New York: Dover, 1975.

Parker, Ann, and Neal, Avon. *Molas: Folk Art of the Cunha Indians*. New York, Clarkson N. Potter, Inc., 1977.

Petrie, Flinders. *Decorative Patterns of the Ancient World for Craftsmen*. New York: Dover, 1974.

Pro Helvetia Foundation. *Swiss Folk Art*. Zurich: German Arts Council, 1968.

Pronin, Alexander. *Russian Folk Arts*. Cranbury, New Jersey, A. S. Barnes and Co., Inc., 1975.

Stasoy, V. *Russian Peasant Design Motifs for Needleworkers and Craftsmen*. New York: Dover, 1976.

III. HISTORICAL REFERENCES

Alford, Lady Marian M. *Needlework as Art.* London: EP Publishing Ltd., 1975. Reprinted from 1886 edition.

Bruhn, Wolfgang, and Tilke, Max. *A Pictorial History of Costume.* New York: Hastings House Publishers, 1955.

Colby, Averil. *Quilting.* London: B. T. Batsford, 1972.

Conn, Richard. *Robes of White Shell and Sunrise.* Denver, Colorado: Denver Art Museum, 1974.

Fairservis, Walter A., Jr. *Costumes of the East.* New York: American Museum of Natural History, 1971.

Hope, Thomas. *Costumes of the Greeks and Romans.* New York: Dover, 1962.

Kohler, Carl. *A History of Costume.* New York: Dover, 1963.

Miles, Charles. *Indian and Eskimo Artifacts of North America.* Chicago: Henry Regnery Co., 1963. Bonanza Book Edition.

Osborne, Lilly de Jongh. *Indian Crafts of Guatemala and El Salvador.* Norman, Oklahoma: University of Oklahoma Press, 1965.

Robinson, Stuart. *A History of Dyed Textiles.* Cambridge, Massachusetts: The M.I.T. Press, 1969.

———*A History of Printed Textiles.* Cambridge, Massachusetts: The M.I.T. Press, 1969.

Swain, Margaret H. *Historical Needlework: A Study of Influences in Scotland and Northern Ireland.* New York: Charles Scribner's Sons, 1970.

Tilke, Max. *Costume Patterns and Designs.* New York: Hastings House Publishers, 1974.

Supplies

Generally, your needlework, craft shops, and specialty sources for fibers and sewing needs will carry necessary materials. You will find suppliers advertised in various hobby publications, more than we have room to list here. Many are mail-order and will provide catalogs when you send them a postcard. If a charge is required, they will inform you. Refer to special needlework editions of magazines on your newsstand, in the library, or from subscriptions such as *McCall's, Woman's Day, Ladies Circle, Vogue, Fiberarts, Creative Crafts, Embroiderer's Journal,* and so forth.

For unusual items mentioned in the text, the following will be helpful.

Folkwear (Patterns for Clothing)
Box 98
Forrestville, California 95436

Igolochkoy (Russian Punch Needle)
P. O. Box 818
Palo Alto, California 94302

Index

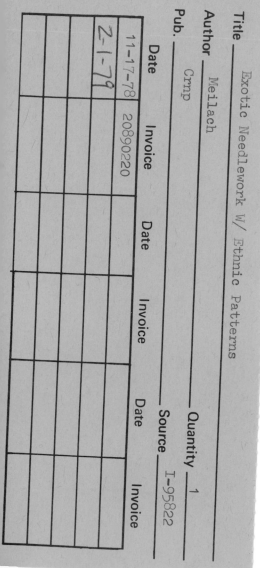

Title _____ Exotic Needlework W/ Ethnic Patterns

Author _____ Meilach

Pub. _____ Crmp

Date	Invoice	Date	Invoice	Date	Invoice
11-17-78	20890220				
2-1-79					

Quantity ___ 1

Source ___ I-95822